HARD CHOICES

Social Democracy in the Twenty-First Century

Christopher Pierson

Polity

First published in 2001 by Polity Press
in association with Blackwell Publishers Ltd

Editorial office:
Polity Press
65 Bridge Street
Cambridge CB2 1UR, UK

Marketing and production:
Blackwell Publishers Ltd
108 Cowley Road
Oxford OX4 1JF, UK

Published in the USA by
Blackwell Publishers Inc.
350 Main Street
Malden, MA 02148, USA

ISBN 0-7456-1984-3
ISBN 0-7456-1985-1 (pbk)

Library of Congress Cataloging-in-Publication Data
Pierson, Christopher.
    Hard choices : social democracy in the 21st century / Christopher Pierson.
        p. cm.
Includes bibliographical references and index.
    ISBN 0-7456-1984-3 — ISBN 0-7456-1985-1 (pbk)
1. Socialism. 2. Gray, John, 1948– 3. Giddens, Anthony. I. Title.
HX73.P537 2001
320.53′1—dc21
                                                                00-011731

A catalogue record for this book is also available from the British Library.

Typeset in 11 on 13 pt Berling
by SetSystems Ltd, Saffron Walden, Essex
Printed in Great Britain by MPG Books Ltd, Bodmin, Cornwall

This book is printed on acid-free paper.

Contents

Acknowledgements

This book was begun in the School of Politics at the University of Nottingham and finished whilst I was a Visiting Research Professor in the Political Science Program at the Australian National University. I am grateful to both institutions (and their library and administrative staffs) for their support. My work in both Australia and the UK was generously supported by a Research Grant (R000222694) from the Economic and Social Research Council whose assistance I am very happy to acknowledge. Thanks also to the staff at Polity Press who waited patiently for this manuscript to appear. At differing times, and more or less formally, the arguments here were run past friends and colleagues in both Australia and the UK. I am grateful to all those who tried to put me right and especially to Frank Castles, Hilary Morrissey and Lucy Sargisson for their persistence. Of course, the mistakes remain entirely my own.

Chris Pierson

Introduction

Amid the many uncertainties that surround us at the start of a new century, one piece of political 'common sense' attracts surprisingly widespread consent: that, at least in their 'traditional' form, social democracy and its characteristic regime of social protection are 'exhausted'. For some on the right, this is a matter of celebration, to be pressed to an ever more radical dissolution. For others on the traditional left, it is a matter of hand-wringing regret. For those seeking to fracture this traditional political topography and identify radicalism with 'the centre', or indeed to chart a 'third way', it is an opportunity to set a new agenda for economy, welfare and state which will outflank the old arguments about equality and redistribution and put policy on a quite new footing appropriate to a post-political and post-collectivist age. There are two problems with these views: one is to do with misrepresenting the past, the other is to do with misunderstanding the present.

Forgetting is, as Nietzsche (1996, p. 39) observed, a learned skill. But in forgetting, as in remembering, we tend to be rather choosy. In essence, I want to argue that a rather selective memory has led to the debate about the future of social democracy (or its exhaustion) being based upon a quite misleading (and partial) reading of its past (see Bale, 1999). In the first half of the book I attempt, however briefly, to restore some of the complexity to social democracy's past. In the second half of the book, I move on to the present and consider the ways in which a few contemporary half-truths – most crucially those focusing on the impact of a globalized economy and the dynamics of demographic change – have been brought together to justify the abandonment of a range of policy ambitions and instruments which were once seen as the bedrock of a social democratic politics. I do not argue that the old tunes (and policies) continue to be the best, still less that 'nothing has really changed'. In fact, a great deal has changed and policy-makers have to adjust to a range of new circumstances, constraints (and opportunities). But I shall insist that those widely rehearsed accounts which exhort us simply to abandon the 'traditional' terrain of the centre-left have significantly misunderstood what this politics has been about and where it stands now. Social democracy almost always was tricky, a politics of hard choices – and this has not really changed.

Ironically, the business of getting to grips with what social democracy really is (and was) has become more, not less, important in the light of recent changes. For sixty years, Communism was seen as a drag on the Western social democratic tradition, allowing opponents to argue (though always rather selectively) that any infringement of existing property rights or free-market practices was a first step on the long march to Moscow – and a future of repression plus queues. A bipolar world order had obliged social democratic Western Europe to hang on to the American nurse, 'for fear of finding something worse'. Conversely, the Americans were seen to be willing to underwrite a little Western European social largesse as part of the price they paid for maintaining Europe as the front line in the struggle against the red menace. When Soviet communism imploded, however, history seemed to have missed out the 'middle man' and proceeded straight to the consummation of a global liberal capitalism (representative democracy plus shopping malls). As, in their turn, expectations about a self-regulating New World Order have waned – and problems in the operation of a more globalized economy have emerged – the attention of both international and domestic policy-makers has increasingly turned to a reassessment of the possibilities (and limits) of states' (and other actors') intervention in social and economic life. In a context where confidence in neoliberal solutions has waned – both for policy-makers and publics – the focus returns to a politics which intervenes in (and, of course, helps to constitute) but does not unseat market-based economies. Upon one influential account, this is just what social democracy is: seeking 'to regulate and socialise the wealth-creating and directionless economic dynamism of capitalism, not replace it' (Hobsbawm, 1996).

My aim in this short book is certainly not to defend an old orthodoxy in the face of the new. I do, however, want to develop an argument that is rather more careful about what has changed and how – and what the consequences of these sorts of changes (and continuities) might be. An important first step is to be clear about what social democracy really was. This is not quite so straightforward as we might assume – since social democracy has meant quite different things to different people at different times and in different places. In their haste to reach the exciting terrain that lies 'beyond' social democracy, some have been persuaded to offer only a very brief, synoptic and conveniently archaic reconstruction of this history. It is important to be just a little more reflective and sensitive about social democracy's past (if we are to make a reasoned evaluation of its possible futures). In the light of such an appraisal, I turn to an extended assessment of those forces which are most widely held now to have *dissolved* that traditional social democratic option – namely, economic globalization and rapid demographic change. Finally, and in the light of all these considerations, I consider whether social democrats are now best advised to give up, to seek out a 'third way' or to 'adapt to survive'.

1

The Strange Death of Social Democracy

Since I intend to take issue with much of the 'new' thinking that lies 'beyond' traditional social democracy, it would be as well to begin with a definitive statement of the principal position that I aim to challenge. For this I turn to two distinguished professors at the London School of Economics and to five representative texts. The Professor of European Thought, John Gray, is an especially appropriate figure since his own political trajectory from sometime advocate of Thatcherism to theorist of 'communitarian liberalism' represents a highly personal version of the journey to the radical centre (Gray 1993a, 1993b, 1996, 1997, 1998). Anthony Giddens, Director of the LSE, has, after a distinguished and highly productive career as a social theorist, devoted his attention increasingly to mapping the changing political context of late modernity (Giddens, 1990, 1991, 1992, 1994, 1998, 1999, 2000; Giddens and Pierson, 1999). Both men are strongly associated with the idea of a new 'radical centrism' and, more especially in the case of Giddens, with the rather spectral idea of a 'third way'. I take Gray's essays *After Social Democracy* and *False Dawn* and key sections of Giddens's *Beyond Left and Right*, *The Third Way* and *The Third Way and its Critics* as definitive and authoritative statements of this 'post-social democratic' approach.

After social democracy

John Gray's position is seemingly unambiguous: 'Today, we are witnessing the crisis and decomposition of social democracy' (Gray, 1996, p. 24). Although, paradoxically, Gray speaks of the recent period having seen an 'emerging social democratic consensus in Britain', he insists that this impulse, itself a response to the collapse of the neoliberal project, must fail. 'Social democracy was a political project whose stability and even identity depended on the geo-strategic environment of the Cold War' (p. 12). With the unfreezing of this global dispensation, 'the historical context in which social-democratic conceptions made sense has ceased to exist.' More than this, it is 'not only the historic policies but also the constitutive morality of social democracy [that] have been rendered utopian by the ruling forces of the age' (pp. 8, 26). Though eclectic, social democratic thinking is said to have at its core a commitment to 'a form of society-wide egalitarian community'. Whether for epistemological or electoral reasons, such a commitment to 'simple' equality is no longer sustainable. The twin failure of both social democracy *and* neoliberalism provides the context for Gray's own advocacy of a 'communitarian liberal' alternative (which he appears willing sometimes to allow to be described as a 'third way').

What, upon Gray's account, was social democracy and why has it failed? In its essence, social democracy was 'a complex structure of ideas, policies, institutions and objectives embodied in the social and political settlements in a number of west-European countries during the postwar period up to the end of the 1980s' (1996, p. 24). Its roots lie in the late nineteenth- and early twentieth-century revision of classical socialism, especially of its Marxist variant. The most important elements in this revision are said to have been the rejections of nationalization and of central planning of the economy. Social democracy's 'central objectives and policies' were fourfold (p. 25):

- the pursuit of greater equality of income and wealth through redistributive tax and welfare policies;
- the promotion of full employment through economic growth;
- a 'cradle-to-grave' welfare state defended as the social embodiment of citizen rights;

- support for and cooperation with a strong labour movement as the principal protector of worker's interests.

In the postwar period, social democrats appropriated Keynesianism to generate 'a coherent and viable economic programme', a regime which was visited with considerable success at least until the early 1970s. In difficulty from the late 1960s and in crisis after 1973, the failure of the 'Mitterrand experiment' in the early 1980s and the collapse of the Swedish model in the early 1990s provided, for Gray, the clearest evidence that this social democratic era is over. In his later essay *False Dawn*, Gray is quite definitive: 'Global markets . . . make social democracy unviable':

> Social market systems are being compelled progressively to dismantle themselves, so that they can compete on more equal terms with economies in which environmental, social and labour costs are lowest. The question social market economies face is not whether they can survive with their present institutions and policies – they cannot. It is whether the adjustments that are imperative will be made by a further wave of neo-liberal reforms or by policies which harness markets to the satisfaction of human needs. (1998, pp. 99, 92)

How was the viability of social democracy undermined? At the top of Gray's list are changes in the international economy. Thus, he insists that 'it is no exaggeration to say that the global freedom of capital effectively demolishes the economic foundations of social democracy' (1996, p. 26). Among the most important elements in this process of globalization are the emergence of billions of industrious, skilled (and comparatively low paid) workers outside the metropolitan heartlands of social democracy, allied to 'the disappearance of any effective barriers to the global mobility of capital' (p. 12). These trends were greatly accelerated by the end of the Cold War which brought the supply of cheap yet skilled labour to the very doorstep of the Western European heartland of the social democratic welfare state. These changes have brought with them an effective decline in the governing capacities of nation-states (within which the social democratic project was grounded), with a declining capacity to control the parameters of (what have largely ceased to be) domestic economies and increasing difficulties in main-taining the legitimacy and effectiveness of existing taxation regimes (given the increased international mobility of both capi-tal and skilled labour).

Full (male) employment had been a core component of post-war social democracy and its welfare state. Changes in the (domestic and international) economy from the 1970s onwards made this regime increasingly difficult to sustain and rendered the traditional countercyclical measures of social democrats – 'stimulating investment through a policy of deficit-financing' – undoable. At the same time, these deep-seated economic changes began to undermine the pattern of (relatively stable) class forma-tion on which social democracy's political support had been built. 'Insofar as it was embodied in a labourist movement, social democracy is now a political project without an historical agent' (Gray, 1996, pp. 12–13).

Almost as debilitating, upon Gray's account, is the implausibil-ity of social democracy's core ethical commitment to a simple and undifferentiated principle of equality. Just as neoliberalism is undermined by its commitment to an undifferentiated belief in the primacy of individual liberty secured through the unhindered operation of markets, so is social democracy undermined by its 'egalitarian imposition of a single conception of justice in all contexts of economic life'. 'Justice' and 'fairness' are important elements of a good common life, itself a necessary premise of individual flourishing – but they are localized, contextual and will sometimes conflict. Equality is complex, not simple (following Walzer, 1983).

Beyond left and right

Giddens's take on these issues is rather different, but hardly more comforting for defenders of a 'traditionally' social democratic politics. For Giddens, the contemporary problems of social democracy, and the welfare state project with which revealingly he largely identifies it, have to be set in the much broader context of the changing character of late modernity and its corresponding political modalities. For much of modernity, so Giddens argues, to be radical was usually to be some sort of a socialist (even if only a social democratic one!). But at the end of the millennium, with communism and the 'planned economy' consigned to 'the dustbin of history', socialists seem to have been left with little more than the 'conservative' plea to 'defend the welfare state'. While conservation is an important value for Giddens in a world increasingly threatened by ecological disaster, the transformation of modernity through which we are now living requires that radical politics be radically rethought – and this means a whole-sale re-evaluation of the position that the social democratic left (or centre-left) has traditionally maintained. Like Gray, Giddens insists that neoliberalism does not offer a viable alternative. The neoliberal project has collapsed, so Giddens supposes, under the weight of a contradiction at its core. In essence, its attachment to the purgative powers of markets makes it profoundly hostile to tradition, yet its own legitimacy depends on precisely those very traditional ideas and practices (of nation, religion, family and gender) which it systematically undermines. For Giddens, it is this peculiar conjuncture – in which 'socialism and conservatism have disintegrated, and neoliberalism is paradoxical' – that mandates the search for a new radical politics which is 'beyond left and right'.

The broader context for this rethinking of radical politics is defined by four major developments. First, there is the intensification of *globalization*, not just as an economic but also a political and cultural force. Second is the extent to which we now live in a *post-traditional social order* in which nothing can be taken for granted and in which every relationship and every aspect of self-identity is provisional and in some sense 'up for grabs'. Third, our societies are characterized by a growth in *social reflexivity* in which our much more provisional and 'chosen' identities and institutions are constantly monitored and permanently vulnerable to redefinition and reformation. Fourth, all these changes increasingly take place in a context of *manufactured uncertainty* and *manufactured risk*. Life has always been risky and our futures uncertain, but increasingly we can see that these uncertainties are the product not of nature but of (quite often intentional) human intervention in the natural world.

Socialism in its several variants (which, for Giddens, includes 'the Keynesian "welfare compromise"') was the radical politics of a 'simpler', less 'reflexive' modernity and the welfare state was an appropriate mechanism for dealing with external (rather than manufactured) uncertainty:

> The 'class compromise' of welfare institutions could remain relatively stable only so long as conditions of simple modernization held good. These were circumstances in which 'industriousness' and paid work remained central to the social system; where class relations were closely linked to communal forms; where the nation-state was strong and even in some respects further developing its sovereign powers; and where risk could still be treated largely as external and to be coped with by quite orthodox programmes of social insurance. None of these conditions holds in the same way in conditions of intensifying globalization and social reflexivity. (Giddens, 1994, pp. 8, 149)

The new circumstances of reflexive modernity require a much greater emphasis on the active involvement of citizens (as individuals, families or groups) in making their own welfare arrangements in a process of active engagement with the state. They also offer the opportunity to move from a *productivist* society (which Giddens sometimes associates with capitalism) driven by an addiction to economic growth (with its attendant twin compulsions to work and to consume) towards a *post-scarcity order* – not a society of abundance, but a society in which the virtues (and vices) of economic growth are given their proper weight rather than unquestioned primacy. In this context, Giddens calls for a new emphasis on *life politics* – a politics which is about 'how (as individuals and as collective humanity) we should live in a world where what used to be fixed either by nature or tradition is now subject to human decisions' – and *generative politics* – a politics which 'exists in the space that links the state to reflexive mobilization in the society at large . . . a politics which allows individuals and groups to *make things happen*, rather than have things happen to them' (1994, p. 15).

From this follows Giddens's commitment to the idea of *positive welfare*: welfare as the creative, bottom-up, self-activity of citizens and their voluntary associations pursuing greater autonomy and happiness in a 'reflexive engagement with expert systems' (1994, p. 153). Traditional welfare states treated risks as external (as misfortunes, such as ill-health or unemployment, which just happen to people) and its citizens as passive recipients of the state's largesse. They also operated with a set of assumptions about people's lifestyles (full-time lifelong employment for men, childrearing in stable heterosexual marriages for women) which just do not square with the ways we (choose to) live now. Increasingly, so Giddens argues, we have to recognize that social contingencies, such as ill-health, are often the product of individuals' perverse behaviour or neglect (as in the case of smoking or obesity). Remedies lie not just in the hands of the state but in individuals, families and groups exercising 'lifestyle responsibility' (and making themselves happier in the process), often, though not necessarily, in partnership with the state. Given the greater diversity and changeability in individuals' lives (in terms of employment, marital status, household composition and so on) we need welfare arrangements which foster a *politics of second chances* (1994, p. 172). Giddens insists that existing 'passive' welfare states *can* create demoralizing patterns of welfare dependency and social exclusion, arguing, for example, that retirement at sixty-five is an arbitrary imposition of inactivity on a (growing) group of the population which is generally healthy and keen to be economically active (1994, pp. 169–72; 2000, pp. 39–40). What is needed is a welfare regime which is empowering, which provides the opportunities (and sometimes the resources) to enable individuals to take responsibility for their own well-being.

What would a positive welfare regime look like? Giddens is not prescriptive (since positive welfare is supposed to be permissive rather than obligatory), but he does have a number of indicative suggestions:

> [Systems of welfare in a post-scarcity order] would have to escape from reliance on 'precautionary aftercare' as the main means of coping with risk; be integrated with a wider set of life concerns than those of productivism; develop a politics of second chances; create a range of social pacts or settlements, not only between classes but between other groups or categories in the population; and focus on . . . a generative conception of equality. (1994, p. 182)

He envisages a series of social pacts (between rich and poor or between the sexes, for example) in which both sides would trade off something with the other (in terms of employment opportunities or childcare responsibility, but not, so Giddens insists, wealth) in order to yield a positive-sum welfare gain for both parties. In substantive terms, he envisages a greater emphasis upon health promotion, a larger role for private pensions and the targeting of benefits and the abolition of statutory retirement (1994).

Giddens and *The Third Way*

Something of a shift occurs between *Beyond Left and Right*, published in 1994, and Giddens's more directly political essays *The Third Way* (1998) and *The Third Way and its Critics* (2000). The spectre of a 'third way' (at this juncture still to be plotted between communism and capitalism) appears but briefly in the earlier text. Here it is identified with market socialism, a hybrid form which is fairly summarily dismissed (1994, pp. 68–9). With *this* third way abandoned, Giddens concluded in his earlier work that 'the history of socialism as the avant-garde of political theory comes to a close.' The tone (and the coordinates) of Giddens's later essays are a little different, certainly more cautious. Now it appears that social democracy can in fact 'not only survive but prosper'. Indeed, it turns out that the third way is synonymous with both 'the modernizing left' and 'modernizing social democracy'. But this redemption of the politics of the left is possible only if 'old-style or classical social democracy (the old left)' is abandoned. For Giddens, the key defining characteristics of this 'old-style' social democracy are these:

- Pervasive state involvement in social and economic life.
- State dominates civil society.
- Collectivism.
- Keynesian demand management, plus corporatism.
- Confined role for markets; the mixed or social economy.
- Full employment.
- Strong egalitarianism.
- Comprehensive welfare state, protecting citizens 'from cradle to grave'.
- Linear modernization.
- Low ecological consciousness.

- Internationalism.
- Belongs to bipolar world.

The newer third way which Giddens discusses and, in the end, wants to recommend, is to be found in the space that lies 'beyond' both this 'old-style' social democracy and its neoliberal rival. As outlined in *The Third Way* (1998, pp. 7, 66, 70), its key values are:

- Equality.
- Protection of the vulnerable.
- Freedom as autonomy.
- No rights without responsibilities.
- No authority without democracy.
- Cosmopolitan pluralism.
- Philosophic conservatism.

The most important programmatic elements are:

- The radical centre.
- The new democratic state (the state without enemies).
- Active civil society.
- The democratic family.
- The new mixed economy.
- Equality as inclusion.
- Positive welfare.
- The social investment state.
- The cosmopolitan nation.
- Cosmopolitan democracy.

So baldly stated, it might seem that many of the key values and policy ambitions of the 'new' social democracy, give or take the odd ecological imperative, follow rather seamlessly from the 'old'. After all, 'traditional' social democracy was also centrally concerned with securing equality and the protection of the vulnerable. It also countered the politics of neoliberalism with an appeal to freedom as effective autonomy. But Giddens is keen to develop these core principles in ways which he sees as quite different from the traditional apparatus of social democracy. Redistribution remains important, but upon Giddens's account we should be moving from the traditional redistribution of resources towards the 'redistribution of possibilities'. Equality is still a key value, but it is now to be understood as a part of the politics of *inclusion* (equality of civil and political citizenship, equal *access* to employment and educational *opportunities*). At the same time, 'it is no good pretending that equality, pluralism and economic dynamism are always compatible', and just a little more inequality and a little more economic insecurity may be the price of a dynamic and risk-taking economy. In the field of social welfare, Giddens is still more stringent. The 'traditional' social democratic welfare state is seen to 'create almost as many problems as it resolves' (1998, p. 16). While he defends a continuing (if reduced and changed) role for the state in securing individuals' well-being, existing welfare states are seen to be too often bureaucratic, illiberal, dependency-creating and inefficient. Characteristically, they are criticized for having failed to match rights with responsibilities.

Hay and the 'retreat' from social democracy

Both Gray and Giddens have some insightful things to say about the present dilemmas of radical politics and the difficulties of existing welfare state regimes. They voice some prescient criticisms of abiding weaknesses in the wider social democratic tradition. Nonetheless, I believe that, in the end, neither Giddens nor Gray really get the measure of the social democratic predicament (or of its continuing strengths), and consequently that the reconceptualization of 'radical politics' which they recommend is in large part misconceived. At the same time, there are very real problems with resisting this shift towards the 'radical centre' from within the parameters of a social democracy 'traditionally' conceived. We can identify some of these problems by focusing on the trenchant defence of a more traditional social democratic politics mobilized by Colin Hay (1997, 1998, 1999, 2000). Hay is no 'palaeolabourite' but he does firmly resist the trend towards 'modernization' and 'accommodation', offering a particularly clear and powerful statement of the continuing integrity of a more traditionally social democratic approach.

An important element in Hay's argument is that things just

have not changed in the way that the advocates of a 'modernized' social democracy suppose. Thus, crucially, he insists that social democracy may have been undermined not 'by globalization per se [but rather] by *ideas about* globalization'. Thus, 'the *perception* that globalization brings with it the heightened mobility of investment capital may lead (indeed, may well already have led) social democrats to internalize the preferences of capital and, in so doing, to sacrifice their social democracy on the altar of globalization' (Hay, 2000, p. 151; my emphases). There is certainly some merit in pressing this argument as an antidote to some of the sillier things that have been said about the irresistible tide of globalization. Nonetheless, as I shall argue (in chapter 4 below), it does risk missing some very real and salient changes in the parameters facing social democratic policy-makers, while failing to register that these are changes which do not unambiguously support the position taken by social democracy's 'modernizers'.

There is a second and somewhat broader concern about the way in which Hay approaches the current predicament of social democracy. Having rejected several more 'accommodating' alternatives, Hay defines social democracy around the following:

> (i) a commitment to *redistribution* – to the principle that the distribution of social advantage within any capitalist society at any time can never be equitable and must be addressed through a constant imperative to redistribute . . .

> (ii) a commitment to *democratic economic governance* – to the principle that the market, left to its own devices, can only generate outcomes that are inefficient, inequitable and unacceptable and that, accordingly, the state must take responsibility for market outcomes and for the degree of intervention required to ameliorate their excesses . . .

> (iii) a commitment to *social protectionism* – to the principle that it is the primary responsibility of the state to ensure that its citizens are provided for in terms of health, education and welfare in its broadest sense and across the lifespan. (1999, p. 57)

These can certainly be described as classically social democratic principles – the commitment to modify inequality, to moderate market outcomes and to provide a framework of social protection – and Hay's description is certainly a useful summary of some key social democratic expectations. But there are problems with applying these as a litmus test of what is to count as a social democratic regime. In one sense, and somewhat ironically, these criteria are too modest. Since all governments in advanced democratic states intervene to moderate the distributional consequences of initial market incomes, and virtually none leave markets beyond the scope of government regulation, these cannot in themselves be the defining characteristics of a social democratic government. But, at the same time and on a slightly different reading, Hay's criteria can appear to be too demanding as a benchmark of social democratic governance. No social democratic government has ever acted in the belief that, since outcomes in a capitalist society will *always* be inequitable, it must prosecute the 'constant imperative to redistribute' to the point where there is equality of income for all citizens (or a distributional profile that reflects the pattern of citizens' needs). Similarly, the responsibility of social democratic governments for market outcomes has almost never been taken to warrant the straightforward direction of labour and capital (indeed 'Keynesian steering' was often and quite explicitly presented as an *alternative* to planning in the conventional sense of a 'planned economy'). Again, while social protection has been a key ambition of social democratic governments (among others), it has not always and definitively taken primacy over, for example, national defence or economic growth. As ever, and as one might anticipate, social democratic governance in these areas is a *matter of degree*.

Perhaps still more of a problem is that Hay's account of what social democracy is relies so heavily on the politics of *reaction* – *re*distributing wealth or *re*allocating life chances. Much (though not all) social democratic practice lies behind this usage. But, of course, social democratic states (like others) are also centrally involved in the process of *constituting* markets and their outcomes. The crucial issue in the politics of inequality (or welfare) is not whether the state *re*distributes resources and opportunities but rather the final pattern of the income distribution or welfare opportunities themselves and the part that social democratic forces play in promoting these. Constructing markets in ways that squeeze income distributions (or pattern welfare opportunities) – a key component of a 'supply-side' social democracy – may be functionally the equivalent of redistributing the product of less equitable markets or social practices, but it is action which is very partially captured by Hay's definition. Of course, this distinction is not very consequential if we have circumstances in which governments are simply doing less of the same. Although the responsibility for such retrenchment is a separate issue, we do at least then have a metric for saying that such a government is 'less social democratic' (or perhaps just less successful or even less lucky). But it is actually much less clear that a government which presides over lessened income inequality but does not achieve this outcome through *re*distribution constitutes a 'less social democratic' regime. As we shall see, in rapidly changing circumstances, the possibility of doing social democratic things 'by other means' attains considerable importance.

Considering these three responses to the contemporary social democratic predicament may help to locate my own approach in this book. I shall not argue that social democracy is everywhere in fine fighting shape, still less that it does not need to change. I shall argue, however, that the sorts of changes advocated by Gray and Giddens are premised, at least in part, on a misreading of the history of social democratic movements and a misunderstanding of the problems that they (and others) now face. I do so, though, not on the basis that seems to underpin Colin Hay's critique – that there is a particular stipulative basis to social democracy which current reformers are either ignoring or, at worst, 'betraying'. Rather, I shall argue that social democracy is actually a much more diverse and, perhaps surprisingly, interesting tradition than both its detractors and many of its admirers have imagined. I shall argue that some space for a social democratic politics certainly still exists but that, while many of its manifestations need to be defended against those who have bought rather more of the neoliberal story than the evidence will justify, in some areas we do need to think quite differently about what is to be done and how.

I begin by trying to establish a little more carefully just when and what social democracy has been.

2

The Making of Social Democracy

An obstinate will to erode by inches the conditions which produce avoidable suffering, oppression, hunger, wars, racial and national hatred, insatiable greed and envy.

Leszek Kolakowski

The suppression of the abuses of capitalism instead of the suppression of capitalism itself.

Rosa Luxemburg

The only political force of the left that can demonstrate a record of reforms in favor of workers.

Adam Przeworski

Both Gray and Giddens operate with a rather perfunctory account of social democracy. Indeed, Giddens does not really distinguish social democracy from a set of more general criticisms (and strengths) attributed generically to socialism (though he does discuss T. H. Marshall and Tony Crosland as exemplars). For Gray, the roots of social democracy lie in turn of the century revisionism, with its most important manifestation being found in the postwar settlements within Western Europe. For both thinkers, social democracy is an amalgam of practice and ideas, perhaps halfway to being an ideology. According to Giddens, in its traditional form it has become exhausted above all because in terms of both economic management and welfare its modus operandi is top-down or 'cybernetic'. It is the progressive politics of simple modernity. For Gray, it falls victim to the twin processes of global economic change and the declining conviction of universalist, 'simple' conceptions of equality. In Hay's rather different treatment, social democracy is constructed around three key principles: redistribution, democratic economic governance and social protection.

Yet these typifications do very limited justice to the diversity and ambiguity of the social democratic tradition. Indeed, it is really quite unclear when and what social democracy is or was. It has been, by turns, the name of a party or 'family' of parties, of a (rather amorphous) political ideology, of a political strategy (or rather of a broad range of political strategies), of a governing style, of a regime for the 'mobilization of consent'. At times, what look like social democratic strategies have been pursued by parties and governments that would never have described themselves as social democratic. At other times or in other places, Social Democratic parties have pursued policies that are not easily brought within any coherent account of what social democratic politics is (unless that definition is, following Herbert Morrison's infamous if apocryphal example, just whatever any Social Democratic party happens to do). Until we have resolved (or at least explored) this issue, it is extremely difficult to know what it means either to say that social democracy is 'exhausted' or that it has been 'abandoned'.

The Socialist International

A rather obvious, but not altogether helpful starting point lies in the rubric of the Socialist International. With its origins in the split from the Leninist communist parties in the 1920s and 'reconstituted' at the Frankfurt Conference of 1951, the Socialist International is the institutional expression of the global 'family' of parties committed to a rather hazily defined 'democratic socialism'. Membership (which currently extends to 131 parties and organizations) has long been taken as a key indicator of social democratic status (if not of much else). The *Declaration of Principles of the Socialist International* (adopted at the 1989 Stockholm Congress and updating *The Aims and Tasks of Socialism* endorsed at Frankfurt in 1951) is extremely vague (Socialist International 1999). Although socialism rates a mention in the opening statement, thereafter the declaration is rather bolder in its affirmation of democracy and 'solidarity'. It cannot really be said to commit anyone to anything. True to its social democratic lineage, the *Declaration* largely eschews ideology but, even in its anodyne generality, it does point towards a number of characteristic prejudices in the social democratic 'climate of opinion'. These include an endorsement of freedom and justice in terms (of rights and opportunities) with which few liberals could take issue and a celebration of solidarity not as the special quality of socialist politics but as the generic ambition of 'all major humanist traditions'. The *Declaration* is unusually stipulative in its endorsement of the right to 'full and useful employment in an adequately rewarded job', but its commitment to 'socialisation and public property within the framework of a mixed economy' is rather indeterminately glossed. If not quite 'in principle, unprincipled', certainly social democracy as represented by the *Declaration* could be described as 'dogmatically undogmatic'.

The *Declaration* gives us a sense of just how amorphous is social democracy's self-definition, of how conventional is that account of democracy to which it repeatedly commits itself and of how much it is still defined by its historic (but now archaic) mission of marking off the parties of democratic socialism from the 'illegitimate' Communist tradition (a task which, of course, long predates the emergence of the 'Cold War'). But this still tells us comparatively little about the substantive nature of social democracy or the character of its 'exhaustion'. For this, we need to enter into a selective archaeology of social democratic ideas and practices.

Beginning in the middle

Rather than begin our search at the very beginning, it may be more useful to set out from what is often seen as the high water mark of social democracy in its 'golden age' after 1945. It is clearly this image which critics have most frequently in mind when they think of social democracy's decline and fall. Still one of the clearest typifications of social democracy in this period is that furnished by Mark Kesselman. According to Kesselman, the following are the leading shared characteristics of this social democracy:

> First, an acceptance of a capitalist economy is coupled with extensive state intervention to counteract uneven development. Second, Keynesian steering mechanisms are used to achieve economic growth, high wages, price stability, and full employment. Third, state policies redistribute the economic surplus in progressive ways, through welfare programs, social insurance, and tax laws. And, finally, the working class is organized in a majority-bent social democratic party closely linked to a powerful, centralized, disciplined trade-union movement. (1982, p. 402)

This is clear and compelling and it combines 'objectives and policies' in the way that Gray anticipates. It is, however briefly, a description of a 'regime' rather than just a party or even a programme. Mercifully, it is not a 'project'. But we should still see it as a highly stylized account of a very particular kind of social democracy, what we might call the 'classical' postwar social democratic model of governance. Not every postwar social democratic regime corresponded even approximately to this model (perhaps not even the cases of France and Sweden that Kesselman considered). Nor is it clear that social democratic aims *have* to be secured through just these means. Indeed, historically this was *not* what many earlier social democrats had anticipated.

Social democracy as revisionism

In fact, in the period of which Kesselman writes, social democracy had already been around for at least half a century and had had its own eventful history of triumphs (mostly electoral) and disasters (largely associated with its rather dismal failure to contend with either Bolshevism or fascism). For much of the nineteenth century, 'social democrat' was a label that could be attached to anyone who supported the claims of both social ownership and democratization. It defined a radical political position committed to social and political change. Both Marx and the revolutionary party to which Lenin belonged could be called 'social democratic'. The term began to acquire more of its contemporary sense, as Gray recognizes, with the revisionist debates in turn of the century Marxism, and more particularly in the arguments of Eduard Bernstein. In part, this was precisely a struggle about what social democracy could and should be and about what Social Democratic parties could and should do.

The story of Bernstein's 'revision' of Marx and the feverish debate it engendered in turn of the century German Social Democracy has been frequently told (Gay, 1952; Pierson, 1986; Bernstein, 1993; Steger, 1997). Seemingly the key issue for contemporaries – at least for the party's leading players – was whether capitalism was going to be (more or less imminently) overwhelmed by economic catastrophe, as the theoretical sections of the SPD's founding Erfurt Programme of 1891 had seemed to suggest. Bernstein rejected such a prospect, arguing that Marx's anticipations about the future development of capitalism – especially as these had been laid out in the *Communist Manifesto* – had now been empirically refuted. The 'possessing' and 'middle' classes were not diminishing, nor were the wage earners being reduced to a homogenized and impoverished mass. While there were signs of the concentration and centralization of capital, there was at the same time evidence of 'the continuation and renewal of small and medium-sized businesses', and while capitalism remained vulnerable to cyclical fluctuations and recurrent crises, there was no reason to expect a catastrophic collapse (Bernstein, 1993).

Much of the vigorous exchange that Bernstein's views occasioned with the defenders of Marxist 'orthodoxy' – above all, Karl Kautsky and Rosa Luxemburg – centred on the nature of the catastrophe that was (or in Bernstein's view, was not) going to engulf capitalism. The most salient parts of Bernstein's argument for the emergence of a recognizably 'modern' social democracy lay elsewhere – in the political conclusions that he drew from the implausibility of Marx's political economy. Crucially (if somewhat naively) Bernstein sought to replace Marx's supposition that the logic of social change was dialectical with the belief that it was, in essence, evolutionary. Capitalism must still give way to socialism, but such a change might be gradual and incremental. It certainly did not require, as Luxemburg supposed, 'the hammer blow of revolution' (Luxemburg, 1970).

Crucial to this shift was Bernstein's commitment to the epochal significance of the growth of democracy. At the time that Bernstein was writing, the universalization of the suffrage was still a very partial achievement, even for men in Western Europe. But he clearly saw in it the wave of the future: 'politically, in all the developed countries, we are seeing the privileges of the capitalist bourgeoisie giving way to democratic institutions.' With the growth of democracy, 'a social reaction has set in against the exploitative tendencies of capital' (1993, p. 2). Given the almost Jacobin enthusiasm that certain social democrats were later to show for the supremacy of parliament, it is worth noting that Bernstein advocated the extension of democracy in a range of institutions – especially in local government (where extension of the franchise often came earlier) and in trade unions and cooperatives. At the same time, Bernstein was not an enthusiast for democracy as 'pure majoritarianism' – the position that Kautsky (1920, 1964) was later to adopt as giving proper expression to the unqualified rule of the presumed-to-be majoritarian working class (and underpinning the distinction he was to draw between 'dictatorship as a condition' under democratic rules and the 'dictatorship as form of government' which he identified with Bolshevism). Indeed, Bernstein appeared to subscribe to a thoroughly modern and largely liberal-democratic account of democracy as 'majority rule plus minority rights'. He may even have supposed, as have many liberals subsequently, that an apparatus of civil rights is even more important than the share in political power which the universal vote brings.

In fact, Bernstein went still further in this direction. He (just about) retains the idea of transition from a capitalist to a socialist society – but insists that the winning of democracy (and this not only in the representative assemblies of the local and central state) itself transforms the nature and prospects of such a change. First, democracy cannot (for very long) be the agency of class rule: 'In principle, democracy is the abolition of class government, although it is not yet the actual abolition of classes' (1993, p. 143). Nor is it properly the aspiration of Social Democracy to found a proletarian democracy: 'It does not want to replace a civil society with a proletarian society but a capitalist order of society with a socialist one.' Its key aspiration is 'to raise the worker from the social position of a proletarian to that of a citizen (*Burger*) and thus to make citizenship universal' (p. 146). Furthermore, democracy proves to be not just the means of securing a (gradual and non-convulsive) transition to socialism – it is the form taken by socialism itself: 'Democracy is both means and end. It is a weapon in the struggle for socialism, and it is the form in which socialism will be realised' (p. 142).

This touches on one of the enduring ambiguities of social democratic politics. Was socialism supposed to be the same thing as democracy (and, if so, democracy of what kind and in which areas of social and economic life)? Clearly, all social democrats are committed in some way to the interdependence of democracy and socialism. For some, it is principally a question of legitimacy: only so much socialism as can gain a democratic mandate (though often with the further assumption that, given the nature of workers' interests and their numerical strength, the answer to how much will be 'lots'). For others, since both socialism and democracy are about securing equality, they are at least mutually constituting, if not just the same thing. Of course, the democracy so identified may be more or less extensive (does it include the institutions of economic life or, for a rather later generation, family life?) and more or less intensive (direct or representative? based on delegation or representation?). It may be that the compression of social and economic inequalities – even the social ownership of all society's resources – is stipulated as a precondition for the development of democracy. But it does suggest that a social order which is not democratic (in whatever is seen to be the required sense) is not socialist, whatever its pattern of ownership. To this extent, social democrats have been repeatedly driven away from accounts of socialism (and, indeed, of capitalism) which focus principally on questions of ownership. This downplaying of ownership was to be quite crucial to the character of later social democratic configurations.

It is, both for Bernstein and for those who came after him, a comparatively short distance from these views about democracy to the further supposition that socialism is but the latest and most developed expression of the principles of liberalism. According to Bernstein, 'there is no liberal thought that is not also part of the intellectual equipment of socialism . . . one might call socialism "organised liberalism"' (1993, pp. 148, 150; for an interesting parallel and elaboration, see Rosselli, 1994).

More intriguing, though also less clear, are Bernstein's views about the nature of the socialization of production. At this point, Bernstein does not deny that social ownership remains a central part of the social democratic political agenda. Clearly he is not an anarchist; nor does he display much sympathy for syndicalism (as his pronounced preference for consumers' over producers' cooperatives indicates). At the same time, he is acutely aware of difficulties (and dangers) in expropriation through the agency of the centralized state. Apart from the question of 'equity' (Bernstein favours compensating expropriated owners), he insists that it is simply impossible for the public authorities (local or central) to take over even 'the bulk of medium-sized and large businesses'. Following a general socialization of ownership, either such enterprises would have to be leased back to their former owners and managers and/or there would be a catastrophic collapse in production. For the state to seek to direct the process of production centrally would generate 'enforced uniformity and excessive protectionism', which would in turn 'impede or prevent any rational distinction between viable institutions and parasitical institutions'. Bernstein clearly also expects to see labour markets retained (subject to a series of legal protections, including trade union representation and minimum wages and conditions), arguing that 'a right to work, in the sense that the state guarantees everyone employment in his trade, is utterly unlikely to be implemented in the foreseeable future, and it is not even desirable' (1993, p. 150). His rather elliptically expressed alternative to state ownership and the guaranteed 'right to work' is this:

If, on the one hand, the state abolishes all legal obstacles to producers' organisations and transfers certain powers with regard to the control of industry to professional associations, under certain conditions which would prevent them from degenerating into monopolistic corporations, so that full guarantees against wage reductions and overwork are provided, and if, on the other hand, care is taken . . . That nobody is compelled by extreme need to sell his labour under conditions that are unacceptable, then it is a matter of indifference to society whether, in addition to public enterprises and cooperative enterprises, there are enterprises run by private individuals for their own gain. In time, they will of their own accord acquire a cooperative character. (1993, p. 152)

So Bernstein opts for a mixed economy in which state-owned and cooperative enterprises would run alongside private corporations. Strangely, Bernstein offers no further explanation of why private corporations should 'in time . . . acquire a cooperative character'.

Finally, Bernstein insists on reinstating the moral case for socialism (and with it a particular sense of the moral respectability of the working class). Marx was right, so Bernstein supposes, to have confronted the untutored idealism of earlier socialist Utopians, but 'scientific socialism' had itself degenerated into a dogma maintained in the face of empirical evidence (exemplified by a reluctance to recognize rising standards of living among the working population). For Bernstein, it is essential that the objectives of the labour movement 'are inspired by a definite principle which expresses a higher level of economy and of social life as a whole, that they are permeated by a social conception which points to an advance in cultural development and to a more elevated moral and legal standpoint' (1993, p. 209). In abandoning historical materialism, Bernstein rejects what he sees as the chiliastic or Utopian moment in socialist politics. Socialism means a modestly better and improving world – but not a world turned upside down. Its crucial agency lies among 'respectable' and well-ordered workers. The 'purgative' force of revolution – the need to wash away the dross of the preceding social order which was such a central element in defining Luxemburg's attitude to politics – is wholly absent from Bernstein's meliorist account.

Bernstein is an important source of certain key social democratic presumptions: a recognition of Marx's genius allied to a critique of codified Marxism; confidence in the gradual upward trajectory of workers' well-being, fostered by trade unions and underpinned by the legal apparatus of the state; the belief that social reform has fashioned a society which is 'not quite capitalism' any longer; a faith in the capacity to engender gradual change through legal and constitutional reform; an insistence that democracy changes everything and that socialism must have an explicitly moral component. The fusion of socialism with liberalism – socialism as liberalism's further development – is a nearly universal feature of later social democratic advocacy, as is the view that 'Manchester liberalism' is not the epitome but rather the corruption of 'liberalism properly understood'. Bernstein also concerned himself with the question of the appropriate attitude to 'other classes' – in his case, to the small and middling peasantry. He set a pattern in which social democracy has been a politics of class compromise not just with capital, but also with those intermediary classes which classical Marxism had seemingly expected to disappear with capitalism's further development. Bernstein is unusually explicit about just how unsocialist some of these concessions might need to be. The view that social democracy only came to be concerned with the politics of class alliance towards the end of the twentieth century, in the wake of the 'death of the working class', is thus quite misleading (see also Esping-Andersen, 1985, pp. 29–30).

Just as interesting as the classical social democratic themes that are anticipated in Bernstein's work are those ideas of which one can find almost no sign in Bernstein. The role of Bernstein's social democratic state is legal-constitutional rather than economic-corporate – with labour law and trade union rights the principal means of protecting the interests of workers. Bernstein is sceptical about the role of the state – especially the central state – as an owner. Indeed, he seems to argue that, where possible, state enterprises should be in the hands of municipalities rather than the central authorities and, while recognizing an indispensable role for national governments, he envisages a growing role for local government as a more effective medium of democratic governance: 'If democracy is not to outdo centralised absolutism in fostering bureaucracy, it must be based on a highly differentiated system of self-government with the relevant economic responsibilities devolved to all units of government as well as to all adult citizens' (1993, p. 151).

Bernstein has almost nothing to say about economic planning and/or the capacity of governments to direct the macro-economy. He is largely silent on the prospects of the taxation state as a vehicle of redistribution. He is certainly keen on democracy. But this principle is not used to defend parliamentary sovereignty or pure majoritarianism. It is a practice recommended in many areas of social life and is as much about securing a series of individual rights as it is about directing social and economic activity. Reflecting the impact of his encounter with early Fabianism, Bernstein devotes considerable attention to the virtues of consumers' cooperatives: a form which is widely ignored in the later social democratic tradition. He says something (but not much) about the welfare state. Here again, he defends public provision but also municipal or trade union administration of, for example, health and unemployment insurance (1993, p. 183). He is hardly an unyielding advocate of a generous welfare state: 'Simply to demand state maintenance for all the unemployed means giving, not only for those who cannot find work, but also those who refuse to look for work, access to the public trough . . . It really does not take an anarchist to see the endless heaping up of public responsibilities as too much of a good thing' (1993, p. 161). Like T. H. Marshall a generation later, Bernstein emphasizes that new political and industrial rights have to be set against the continuing *responsibility for economic self-reliance* laid on those who are able to work' (1993, p. 149).

Bernstein certainly proves to be an important source of social democratic ideas. Famously he calls at the end of *Evolutionary Socialism* for social democracy to abandon its revolutionary social-ist rhetoric and to recognise itself as a 'democratic, socialistic party of reform' (see 1993, p. 186). Bernstein's politics are reso-lutely reformist but, on closer inspection, his contribution to the development of social democracy is rather more ambiguous. It is certainly hard to cast him as an unqualified apologist of the centralized state, nationalization, planning, 'top-down' social engineering or 'simple' equality (and to this extent his views might be thought to anticipate some key themes in the literature of the Third Way). In so far as these are defining ideas of social democracy, we shall have to seek them elsewhere.

Social democracy as anti-revisionism

Ironically, some of these ideas are rather more prominent in the work of one of Bernstein's leading opponents in the battle over revisionism – the some time 'pope of Marxian orthodoxy', Karl Kautsky. Although Bernstein and Kautsky were to end up occu-pying much the same space in German Social Democracy by the 1920s, at the time of the revisionist dispute Kautsky defended quite a different account of socialism and democracy, one which rested not on the revision but, as Kautsky saw it, the vindication of Marx's historical materialism. In essence, Kautsky argued that Marx had been right about the nature of capitalism's further development. In the face of Bernstein's counterclaims, he insisted that the concentration and centralization of capital had continued, that class struggle had intensified and that a process of ever more crippling crises of capitalism was in motion. The appearance of a growing middle class was both deceptive and temporary.

Democracy was certainly a transformative principle but not at all in the way that Bernstein supposed. Kautsky shared with Bernstein (and, in this instance, with Rosa Luxemburg too) the belief that the securing of civil and political rights – freedoms of association, assembly, the press and the vote – was a vital precondition for the development of an effective workers' political movement. But in contrast to Luxemburg, he argued that once the proletariat gained access, 'parliamentarism begins to change its character.' The ambition of the workers and their party must be to transfer as much political authority as possible to parliament, the most popular-democratic element of the state. Unlike Bernstein, Kautsky did not want to see proletarians transformed into citizens (or, at least, not yet). In his account, parliamentary democracy was the means of prosecuting the intensifying class struggle, which would continue to develop in the ways that Marx had classically anticipated. This 'built-in' majority for the working class which capitalism unavoidably generated, combined with the majoritarianism which was the ruling logic of parliamentarism, would generate the conditions for unmediated rule by the working class, ensuring that 'a genuine parliamentary regime can be as much an implement of the dictatorship of the proletariat as an instrument of the dictatorship of the bourgeoisie' (Kautsky in Salvadori, 1979, p. 37).

A key question for turn of the century leaders of the SPD (and, of course, one of the most polemical issues in the slightly later debate over the Russian Revolution) was this: 'when are the social and economic conditions ripe for a transition to socialism?' For Kautsky, one of the great virtues of parliamentary democracy was that it took the guesswork out of answering this question. A parliamentary majority was a necessary (though not sufficient) condition for transition to socialism, not least because, so he believed, the simple arithmetic of parliamentary elections would help to persuade the old ruling class that their time was up. But just as importantly, Kautsky saw parliamentary democracy as the desirable, indeed as the necessary form of governance under a new and socialist republic. The functions of the state and the bureaucracy are technically indispensable in a modern society (capitalist or socialist). Exercising control over the government is 'the most important duty of parliament and in that it can be replaced by no other institution' for 'the executive can only be supervised by another central body, and not by an unorganized and formless mass of the people' (Kautsky, 1964, p. 26). A socialist government might make the institutions of representative government more accountable but it could not dissolve them in favour of some form of bottom-up self-governance.

Reform or revolution?

This brings us to a key question about the general character of a revisionist social democracy. What was the nature of the change (if any) that it promised? The oft-repeated case against the revisionist social democratic approach was most starkly posed at its origins in Luxemburg's polemic *Reform or Revolution?* (Luxemburg, 1970). In essence, Luxemburg argued that there could be no question of gradual and incremental movement from a capitalist to a socialist society engineered through parliamentary democracy (a necessarily bourgeois form in Luxemburg's account) and the agencies of the existing state apparatus (which needed to be smashed and replaced). In Luxemburg's damning phrase, the strategy of the revisionists would generate 'not the realisation of socialism, but the reform of capitalism . . . the suppression of the abuses of capitalism instead of the suppression of capitalism itself' (1972, pp. 49–50). (Luxemburg's view has continued to underpin the scepticism of several generations of Marxist and neo-Marxist critics of parliamentary socialism; see, *inter alia*, Miliband, 1961; Wiseman, 1996.)

Most of those social democrats who have seen themselves as revisionists of a sort have, at least until the most recent period (symbolically one might say until 1989), taken issue with Luxemburg's criticism. From Kautsky through the Austro-Marxists to André Gorz's advocacy of *autogestion* in France in the 1960s, some social democrats have always depicted themselves as the advocates of 'revolutionary reforms' (Kautsky, 1910; Bottomore,

1989; Gorz, 1967). Sometimes these have been represented as reforms which are inconsistent with the logic of capitalism (and, in this sense, system threatening). Others have been seen as bringing in changes which themselves furnish a 'slow revolution', as in the wage-earners' funds strategy for the incremental sociali-zation of the Swedish economy (see Esping-Andersen, 1985). Others again, perhaps most famously Tony Crosland in *The Future of Socialism* in 1956, argued that the cumulation of social reforms leaves a system which is so changed that it is 'no longer properly called capitalism' (Crosland, 1964). In each case, the transition from capitalism (if not yet into socialism) is seen not as an event but as a process through which fundamental change is, however gradually and undramatically, secured. What we find in many social democratic accounts is not so much an anticipated trajectory from capitalism to socialism but rather the transforma-tion of liberal capitalism into a distinctive and more socialist (because more equal) form of modernity.

The generic issue at stake here is whether reform must always, or at least has always, meant shoring up rather than shuffling off capitalism. Obviously, it is not too difficult to conjure up a case against the reformers (especially if we avoid engaging with the twentieth century's leading counterfactuals) but, given the tick-lish question of definitions, not quite so easy to be sure of a conviction. (Is socialism all about social ownership; if so, what forms count? Is it about equality? if so, how much and of what kind? Is socialism the name for a distinctive form of social organization or for a particular reforming disposition?) Certainly, that rather jaundiced view which holds that social democracy is just the name for a rather spineless form of accommodation to the status quo benefits from 20/20 hindsight. We shall return to the possibilities and limitations of various reformisms later. For now our concern is with what social democracy is/was (not whether it is doomed to disappoint). In such an enterprise, it is surely evident, perhaps almost self-evident, that *reformism* is quite central to the social democratic tradition. And, in so far as social democracy constitutes a coherent political ideology, it seems clear that virtually all of its adherents have held that if its reforms are not system transforming, at a minimum they should 'make a difference', where that difference is something other than simply making capitalism ever more secure. (Although, we should add that achieving social cohesion and avoiding social upheaval have sometimes been seen as legitimate goals of reform not just by social democrats but by some communist parties too, as definitively illustrated by the postwar history of the Italian Communist Party).

Bernstein and his contemporaries were clearly important in articulating some of the ideas that have been seen as definitively social democratic (as well as some which have been more or less quietly forgotten). Focusing on just these sources can, however, give us an image of social democracy which is too 'revisionist' in character. Although most European social democratic parties (outside of Britain) described themselves originally as Marxist in inspiration, and thence defined their social democratic 'repositioning' in terms of a 'revision' of Marx, this gives undue weight to systematic ideas in parties which have characteristically sought to play down their indebtedness to any 'fixed' set of ideas.[1] In the British case, it has long been argued that New Liberalism or even Christian Socialism were much more influential sources of ideas for the reforming left, and indeed, in both Britain and the continent, the appeal to a sometimes rather loosely imagined citizenship has often been seen to be as important a source of social democratic ideas as has Marxism (on the British case see, for example, Orr, 1979). Although breaking with a more 'fundamentalist' past has served an important symbolic function in a range of parties (from the SPD's Bad Godesburg to British New Labour's abandonment of Clause Four), in practice social democratic parties have almost always preferred to define themselves around a very diffuse set of values.

Parties and movements – social democratic ones certainly no less than any others – are also about the formation, articulation, organization and mobilization of interests (see Krieger, 1999). In significant part, social democracy was about giving political representation to newly enfranchised (and largely male) workers and their interests – generally through improving their terms of trade in existing (labour) markets and guaranteeing certain forms of (welfare) provision through the state, rather than by promising an end to wage labour and markets in general. For much of the time this politics was not so much a long march through the institutions as an incremental trudge through the dreary day-to-day business of the 'labour movement'. Certainly, the institutional basis of social democracy quite often developed with precious little thought for its intellectual underpinning.

Social democracy in the age of catastrophe

The Great European Civil War of 1914–1945 was catastrophic for social democracy (as it was, of course, for almost everyone else). The outbreak of war in 1914 dissolved the fragile unity of the socialist 'movement' and the Second International. It destroyed – in both its genteel and more robust variants – the characteristically nineteenth-century belief in general progress towards a more civilized social order. And the outcome of the Bolshevik revolution which helped to shape so much else in the 'short twentieth century' helped to define what social democracy was for half a century to come. Attributing blame for the division of socialist forces after 1917 has been a cottage industry on the left ever since (and there is certainly plenty of blame to go round), but more salient here is what this meant for social democracy. If the 'other' which had helped to unite the broad church of social democratic opinion before 1914 was inter-national capitalism, after 1917 it was joined on the other flank by what Kautsky called the 'Tartar socialism' of the Soviet Union (1920, p. 232). There were repeated attempts to span this divide in the era that followed – from the '2½' International of the Austro-Marxists in the early 1920s, to the long and winding road presented by the 'terza via al socialismo' of the Italian Communist Party (PCI) after 1945.

Some socialists in the West, even those minded to condemn what they knew of the excesses of Stalin's regime, were still impressed by the mighty productive achievements of a planned economy. Others pointed sympathetically to the extraordinary challenge that faced any Russian government and the conspicu-ously unhelpful attitude of the Western allies. But the position of Western social democracy was rarely one of equidistance. Karl Kautsky was only the first among many Western social democratic leaders to argue that if the workers in Western Europe faced a choice between liberal capitalism and Bolshevik socialism they would choose the former – and would be right to do so (1920). This helped to underpin the widespread social democratic judgement that, when push comes to shove, civil and political rights are more important than social ownership. As time went by, social democracy became ever more firmly anti-communist, while Social Democratic parties increasingly defined themselves in opposition to Communist parties (furthering a loathing that was very widely reciprocated). The split between Lenin's Third International and the new Socialist International in the early 1920s helped to define social democracy as a movement committed above all else (and however ironically) to the defence of the institutions of Western liberal (and capitalist) democracy. Indeed, the suspicion of ideological proximity to the communists made social democrats almost the most fervent advocates of these Western liberal values and institutions, a tendency which was reinforced by the electoral requirement to maximize 'product differentiation' within the left. With a few exceptions (perhaps the SPD's *Ostpolitik*), postwar social democracy was to be not just resolutely Atlanticist but often vigorously anti-Soviet in orientation, and many 'progressive' policies, both at home and abroad, were simply ruled out by the geopolitical position of Social Democratic parties in the Cold War. At the same time, much of the fabric of postwar Europe's social democratic settlement (including the welfare state) was reliant on US funding.

Two further problems confronted social democracy in the 1920s and 1930s and helped to shape its development thereafter. The first of these was the scourge of mass unemployment, which often coincided with the emergence of the first (and often minority) social democratic governments. Although international experience was varied, perhaps only Sweden's Social Democrats can be said to have fashioned an effective response to this challenge. Others, notably the British Labour Party and still more disastrously Germany's Social Democrats, failed rather conspicuously to address this economic challenge, leaving themselves vulnerable to opponents on both right and left. Throughout the 1930s, those more orthodox Marxists who foresaw a crisis of capitalism and an accompanying intensification of class struggle did not seemingly have to search too hard for pertinent examples.

The second grave disaster to befall social democracy during this period was the rise of fascism. Of course, in many instances these misfortunes were very direct: the elimination of trade union rights, the abolition of normal democratic processes, the imprisonment and murder of leading (and not-so-leading) figures in the labour movement. But the rise of fascism also seemingly dealt a death blow to the social democratic worldview premised on incremental reform, the gradual advance of workers and of their organizations and interests, and the application of reason to achieve modest but steady and unidirectional advances. While some social democrats were undoubtedly driven leftwards by the rise of fascism, of even more lasting importance was the growing commitment across broad swathes of the left in Europe, first, to restore 'normal' capitalism and thereafter to refrain from the sorts of challenges which might reopen the route into fascism. The history of the Italian left and its most important player, the PCI, only makes sense in the context of this priority accorded to avoiding fascism (see Sassoon, 1996).

Of course, it is a mistake to cast the 1930s as a decade of 'loss without limit' for social democracy. Aside from the successes of Swedish social democracy, if there is a social democratic politics in modern America its origins lie in this period. As revisionist accounts of the welfare state have shown, and despite the Depression, this was also an important period in the development of social policy. And, as some postwar social democrats were to remember, the economic problems of the 1930s had a strong regional and sectoral component (which some later governments sought to address).

Conclusion

A number of the most characteristic features of what we recognize as social democratic politics date from this interwar period. Above all else, contemporary social democrats saw the securing (and retention) of parliamentary democratic institutions under universal suffrage as a central and, for many, transformative achievement. There was disagreement about how this popular democracy was to be used to effect social democratic strategies, but accepting the power and integrity of these institutions and recognizing an indissoluble link between achieving social change and promoting *parliamentary* forms of democracy were perhaps the most crucial issues that distinguished social democrats in this period from critics to their left. Committing to parliamentarism also meant signing up to a view of the political process in which parties (which participated in elections with a view to winning them) were central. If socialism embodied ideas that could exist outside the context of any particular party or party regime, the ideas associated with social democracy were always umbilically tied to particular parties (though these did not always function under a 'social democratic' label). In this context, party programmes became the leading vehicle for the dissemination of social democratic ideas (leaving the latter rather general and unsystematic). Given these institutional commitments (and whatever noises about internationalism leaders may have made on suitably auspicious occasions), social democratic ideas were almost always resolutely national in substance. The route march of social democrats was essentially to follow national roads (although the relationship to nationalism was generally much more ambiguous). The commitment to parliamentary democracy and to parties whose central ambitions were parliamentary meant that, from very early on, social democrats sought to broaden their appeal and to pursue social coalitions that went beyond their core working-class constituency. Bernstein's view – that there were not really enough purely proletarian votes to support a successful reforming party – was countermanded from time to time (often reflecting specific party dispositions in particular national contexts) but came to be the predominant social democratic view. Thus the appeal to a broad swathe of 'progressive' sentiment and forces actually goes a long way back in the social democratic tradition.

The status of the change that social democrats sought was ambiguous. Kautsky helped to define a continuing tradition in which parliamentary democracy was seen as the vehicle for pursuing a class struggle the irreconcilable nature of which had been definitively (and rightly) asserted by Marx. But even Kautsky wanted to argue for the continuing integrity of both parliamentary institutions and the public bureaucracy as the necessary future form of a socialist republic. More prominent was the view we may associate with Bernstein, that the winning of popular democracy was the key transformative social change, and that, within that framework, socialism (or 'elements of socialism') could be realized peacefully, gradually and incrementally. Indeed, democratic capitalism was so different from pre-democratic capitalism that it made no sense to apply to it the same criteria and strategies for social change. If this did mean, as the critics of social democracy were extremely keen to insist, a politics of pure accommodation in which even the reformist impulse would eventually fade and die, this was clearly not what Bernstein and the other reformers themselves anticipated. Change, they believed, could be gradual but still profound. This did not so much mean changing patterns of ownership (though they did anticipate changes here) as it did a revaluing of private and public. Anticipating the arguments of Crosland and others, there seems to have been an expectation that public institutions – perhaps corporations but certainly public bureaucracies, educational and cultural facilities, the institutions of an extended citizenship – would redress the balance between private and public powers (while retaining an apparatus of individual rights and obligations). This confidence may now seem misplaced (and there were certainly plenty around at the time who argued that it would prove so to be) but it does seem to have reflected a genuinely held conviction.

At the same time, there are key features of a later and 'classical' social democracy which we do not see in this earlier period. Prominently, the idea that the welfare state or governments' social policy might be the principal vehicle of 'socialist' reform is largely absent from the programmes of parties and individuals in the interwar period. There may have been a case for particular reforms (of unemployment benefits or widows' pensions, for example), but little sense that social policy might in and of itself become the leading embodiment of social change. There is in the 1930s some sympathy with the interventionist economics of Ernst Wigforss and Keynes, but little general sense that the macroeconomy could be effectively controlled by governments. There is evidence of the characteristic 'progressive' scepticism about the anarchic outcomes of markets, and sympathy for what was later and rather unkindly to be styled 'social engineering'. But there is no wholesale commitment to a fully planned economy. With periodic exceptions, nationalization is some way down the order of priorities of social democratic reformers (reflecting a scepticism which is there in Bernstein and even Kautsky).

Finally, we need to observe that overlaying all these programmatic elements is a sense that social democracy is, above all, the name for a political practice, one intimately tied to the hopes (and experiences) of specific (and context-bound) parties. With varying degrees of intimacy Social Democratic parties grew up alongside distinctive national labour market institutions – in relationships that helped to change both. Wherever it ended up, social democracy is largely a European creation and, as such, it was repeatedly shaped and refashioned by the history of the first and cataclysmic half of the twentieth-century.

3

'Classical' Social Democracy and the Alternatives

The (golden) age of social democracy?

For many commentators (and this certainly includes both Gray and Giddens) the 'real' story of modern social democracy begins in 1945. This view is understandable, above all, but not exclusively, for those whose principal focus is on Britain. After the generally dismal experience of labour movements in the 1930s, parties of the left (including communist parties) were widely involved in the reform administrations of the immediate postwar period across Western Europe. In the UK, the Labour Party, returned to government in 1945 with a huge majority, embarked on a series of reforms in education and welfare, including the inauguration of the National Health Service in 1948. The new Labour government was pledged to support full (male) employment and to a series of strategic nationalizations (including the coal industry, which had been a symbol of class conflict and reverses for labour throughout the 1920s and 1930s). There were parallel developments across much of Western Europe and beyond (C. Pierson, 1998a, p. 131). As is now widely recognized, there was plenty of continuity to counterbalance the sense of change in these years. In Britain, as elsewhere, important elements of the welfare state were already well established. There had been moves (albeit not very successful) to develop the informal tripartite mediation of industrial relations before the outbreak of the Second World War, and the 1920s and 1930s saw a succession of texts from most parts of the political mainstream (including the Liberals' Yellow Book and Macmillan's Middle Way) which called for a mixed economy and greater government intervention in industrial and social affairs (see Middlemas, 1979).

But this is still a crucial phase in our story, not just because of the significant changes that social democrats were able to realize during these years but also because, as an object of contemporary and later contemplation (and generalization), this period is quite central to the ways in which social democratic politics is understood (not least, as we have seen, by Gray and Giddens). In the English-speaking world at least, recollections of the leading ideas of this postwar period – the patrician liberalism of Keynes and Beveridge, the meliorist social liberalism of Tom Marshall and, above all, the super-confident reformism of Tony Crosland – still dominate contemporary conceptions of what social democracy is (Plant, 1996). The 'successes' of the period – sustained economic growth, full employment, the building of an extensive welfare state – are frequently contrasted both with what went before and with what was to come after. As such, they feed directly into contemporary accounts of why the social democratic 'project' is in so much trouble (for a characteristic treatment in the context of New Labour, see Driver and Martell, 1998).

At the same time, making sense of the postwar experience is not always easy. In part, this is because the 'reality' of social democracy is itself so diffuse and unclear. But it is also because this is a history with which we seem to be *too* familiar and which we seem to know only *too* well. Even the most nimble-footed of interpreters find themselves wading through the alluvium of several generations of 'popular' and academic accounts of what postwar social democracy is – 'the Middle Way', 'the hyphenated society', the postwar consensus, Butskellism, corporatism, the Keynesian welfare state, 'the future that doesn't work', 'tax and spend'. Accounts of social democracy in this period have acquired an almost canonical status as the embodiment of what social democracy really is, and this presents a particular problem as we try to think about the ways in which social democracy might now be either 'exhausted' and/or 'reconstructed'.

'Keynes-plus-modified-capitalism-plus-welfare-state'

Keynes – as icon if not always as economist – is at the heart of the most influential of these accounts of postwar social democracy and, at the same time, of those stories that social democrats have told themselves about what they were doing and why. While his intellectual heritage has been very widely contested, the key function of Keynes in this account is relatively uncomplicated but, at the same time, quite central to social democracy's self-justification. For social democrats, Keynesianism promised 'political control over economic life' – a change which is absolutely crucial to Crosland's revisionism, for example (Skidelsky, 1979, p. 55; Crosland, 1964). Even those who retained a more Marxian-revisionist framework (like the Swedish Social Democrats) celebrated the economic power that new policy instruments delivered into the hands of reforming governments (see Tilton, 1990). Famously, Keynes's argument was not with capitalism but with those neoclassical economists who believed that capitalist markets, *left to themselves*, would always yield optimal outcomes, including the productive employment of all available labour. But, Keynes insisted, markets did *not* guarantee such equilibrium at full employment. This balance could only be secured *outside* the market. It was the duty of the state to intervene directly in the economy to shape both the propensity to consume and the incentive to invest, so as to ensure that there was sufficient economic activity to utilize all available labour and thus to secure market equilibrium *at full employment*. A whole series of policy instruments – including taxation, public works, monetary policy and the manipulation of interest rates – would assist the interventionist government in discharging this duty. According to Keynes:

> It is not the ownership of the instruments of production which it is important for the state to assume. If the state is able to determine the aggregate amount of resources devoted to augmenting the instruments and the basic rate of reward to those who own them, it will have accomplished all that is necessary. (1973, p. 378)

Such a claim can be seen as quite central to the self-justification of postwar social democratic practice. It was this above all that enabled social democrats to be able to claim to have overcome 'Przeworski's dilemmas' (see Przeworski, 1985).[1] If the state can control the overall pattern and level of investment *and* manipulate the distributional outcomes to which this investment gives rise, the issue of private or public ownership becomes purely technical or pragmatic. With this move, the problem that had loomed so large for social democrats of Bernstein's generation (and which had been constantly raised by their critics), namely, how could 'the expropriation of the expropriators' be realized through the mechanism of representative democracy, simply 'withered away'.

Almost more important to the social democrats' 'spiriting away' of the traditional problem of expropriation was the magic of economic growth (with Keynes again evoked as the leading conjuror). Class confrontation could be avoided and 'progressive' social change achieved if everyone was a winner. The social democratic ambition was to load the dice (a little) in favour of those with the fewest chips. Significant differentials of wealth and income might still have to be tolerated as the price of free institutions and a dynamic economy. But, in time, improvements in the incomes of those at the bottom – allied to an extension of high quality public services – would mean that the wealth of those at the top of the profile would yield less and less real economic and political power. Indeed, great accumulations of wealth would largely serve to gratify the vanity of the wealthy – a petty vice which the rest of society could tolerate. Social democratic opinion (rather than practice) could be tough on unjustified inequalities of wealth – especially on inherited wealth – but, in the larger picture, it was essentially incremental growth that would do most of the work of economic transformation (Crosland, 1964, pp. 224–46).

Dovetailing with this first commitment to Keynesianism, but almost more important in securing the social democratic identity, was the enthusiasm for a 'progressive' social policy and a much-expanded public sector. In fact, governments had for a long time intervened in the regulation of labour markets, the administration of schooling and the maintenance of public health. What distinguished the postwar welfare state (in the eyes of its advocates) was that it would make a virtue of public provision, that it would subordinate the logic of charity to the logic of citizenship and that it would explicitly seek to redistribute both income and life chances in the interests of those who were least favoured by unmediated market outcomes. There was a widespread belief that public administration would also yield greater efficiency and uniformity of provision (compared with the patchy and disorderly regime of semi-voluntary services). In their headier moments, social democrats believed that in time the quality of public services would render private and market-determined alternatives irrelevant (Crosland, 1964). To adopt a later terminology, large areas of social provision would be 'decommodified' – that is, taken outside the realm of the market (Esping-Andersen, 1985). With everyone (who wanted one) in a job, the remaining work of income redistribution would come through progressive taxation (rather than transfers), while social equality would be enhanced (and class divisions attenuated) by the provision of improving public services (financed by economic growth).

It was this combination that came to be described synoptically, and for the most part retrospectively, as the *Keynesian Welfare State*. It invoked a twofold strategy built on active government intervention through (1) the macro-management of the economy to ensure economic growth under conditions of full employment, and (2) a range of social policies dealing with 'the redistribution of the fruits of economic growth, the management of its human effects, and the compensation of those who suffered from them' (Donnison, 1979, pp. 146–50).

A further (often implicit) assumption underlay these social democratic accounts. Although the idea of a postwar 'consensus' has been the subject of a fairly thoroughgoing revision in recent years, it is clear that social democratic accounts of this period did presume some level of agreement about the purposes and institutional underpinnings of the Keynesian welfare state settlement (see C. Pierson, 1998a, pp. 124–8, 154–9). These were not all naive celebrations of an unprecedented outbreak of sweetness and light. Some were clear that both capital and labour (often at the expense of less organized social interests) were consulting their own material well-being in supporting the new order. For others, the compromise was seen to be quite provisional and likely to break down should there be a significant shift in the balance of power between organized labour and capital. It might even be that this was a regime which arose from the very special and depleting stock of collectivist goodwill generated by the unique circumstances of total war. For whatever reason and with whatever degree of stability, social democratic accounts rested on the belief that there was a certain 'mobilization of bias' in favour of 'Keynes-plus-modified-capitalism-plus-welfare-state'. And while there was certainly an assumption among many social democrats that walking the social democratic talk required the coordinated movement of both legs of the labour movement (social democratic party and trade unions), the nature of that relationship varied significantly across a range of examples.

What is more, even where this association with organized labour was seen as indispensable, there was still a belief that there existed a much wider constituency for reform. There was, so social democrats supposed, a more or less stable majority within (what was clearly presumed to be) a national political community, a majority grounded on but by no means confined to organized labour, which would back this gradualist progressivism. In Britain, for example, the faith that social democracy could count 'middle England' among its supporters predates Tony Blair by at least a generation (Donnison, 1979). The operating assumption in this period seems to have been that social democratic parties might lose elections but only to parties that would be willing to uphold a broadly social democratic political agenda.

By the time the first edition of *The Future of Socialism* was published in 1956, the regime which Crosland described as 'Keynes-plus-modified-capitalism-plus-Welfare-State' could be represented as a widely shared background assumption – the secure platform on which more (of generally much the same) could be built: 'To put the matter simply, we have won many important advances; but since we could still have more social equality, a more classless society, and less avoidable distress, we cannot be described as a socialist country' (Crosland, 1964, p. 79). Similarly, T. H. Marshall could be and indeed often was glossed as saying that the institutionalization of social rights in the postwar period had generated a stable and broadly 'progressive' compromise of the tensions between social citizenship and social class (see Marshall, 1963).

'The rise and fall of Keynesian social democracy'

As David Marquand observes (1984), despite the ubiquity of this model as a description of the postwar period, almost no one ever claimed to be a 'Keynesian Social Democrat' and certainly nobody ever went to the barricades or even to the electorate promising 'Keynes-plus-modified-capitalism-plus-welfare-state'. In the British Labour Party, this was what passed for 'modernized socialism', while for its opponents broadly similar assumptions were seen to be the underpinning of 'modern Conservatism'. And yet it is probably not an exaggeration to say that this remains the dominant account of what social democracy is (certainly in the English-speaking academy), most especially (though not exclusively) among those who want to argue that, for good or ill, the social democratic tradition is 'exhausted'. Strangely, too, it was with the supposed 'passing' of this regime that we find its fullest and most explicit typification – an account which, perhaps understandably, was given its clearest expression not by the advocates but rather by the opponents of social democracy (to both right and left).

Undoubtedly, this account draws on some real and sustained historical trends. In contrast to the experience of the 1930s and in defiance of the fears of many that the end of the war would bring renewed economic depression, these were years of fairly full (male) employment, sustained growth in public services and public employment and, above all, the rising affluence associated with sustained economic growth. Indeed, it was the latter which gave most of the scope for social democratic development under whichever party in the postwar years. At the same time, there are plenty of reservations to be voiced about the 'fit' between this model of the postwar social democratic order and the circumstances it was taken to describe. Goran Therborn, for example, argues that the comparative experience of a range of developed states in the period indicates that the logics of Keynesianism and of the welfare state could be quite different (Therborn, 1987). Similarly, there are those who insist that governments' policies in these years could not be persuasively described as 'Keynesian', as well as those who argue that the idea of a sustained 'progressive' social policy regime is equally misleading. As we have seen, even the belief that there existed some sort of postwar consensus has been the subject of a sustained bout of revisionism. And given the importance that is frequently attached to the later electoral difficulties of social democratic parties, it is instructive that many of the most 'golden' years of the Keynesian welfare state were years of Conservative or Christian Democratic rule marked by quite modest growth in public expenditure (van Kersbergen, 1995; C. Pierson, 1998a).

What is still more remarkable, though, is the extent to which this synoptic model of the Keynesian welfare state (or still more briefly, the 'KWS') fed into an elegantly symmetrical account of the postwar world: the rise (1945 to 1970) and fall (1975 onwards) of Keynesian social democracy. In its most familiar form, this is an Anglo-American and neoliberal story. At its simplest, the claim is that postwar social democratic settlements unseated the compelling logic of markets and entrenched the veto powers of special interests, above all, of course, of organized labour. Governments, and the tax burden which went (only) some way towards funding them, grew exponentially. Expanding welfare states punished the innovative and subsidized the indolent. The economic inefficiency and social dysfunctionality which were built into these regimes – and which apparently went unseen through the affluent days of the 1950s and 1960s by all but the most eagle-eyed neoliberals – eventually manifested themselves in the economics of stagflation and a political crisis of governmentality in the 1970s. We are, so it is suggested, still living with the consequences of our rather half-hearted response to this challenge.

Although the polarities are reversed, a similar time-frame underpins many leftist accounts of the postwar social democratic experience. To take one influential example, Bob Jessop has written of the (ideal) typical transition from Keynesian welfare state to Schumpeterian workfare state (Jessop, 1994). Although most attention has been focused on the characteristics of the emergent Schumpeterian workfare state – with its emphasis on governments' promotion of national 'competitiveness' and flexibility in a global economy, with a social policy regime to match – the account relies quite as heavily on the other element in Jessop's account, that is, the 'Keynesian welfare state'. In Jessop's regulationist account, the Keynesian welfare state is seen to have had two key functions: (1) to secure full employment in relatively closed national economies primarily through demand-side management, and (2) to regulate collective bargaining and promote consonant forms of collective consumption. Although Jessop's explanatory framework is quite different from that of the neoliberals (whose own account of this process he keenly contests), he shares with them the supposition that the older regime is brought to a point of crisis by 'its stagflationary impact on the Fordist growth dynamic [and] its growing fiscal crisis rooted in the ratchet-like expansions of social consumption expenditure' (1994, p. 27).

The 'problem' here is not so much with these accounts themselves, which do reflect on some real (if less wholesale than imagined) changes. The real difficulty is twofold: first, that the postwar political order often comes to be identified with social democracy *tout court* (in such a way that the difficulties of this regime are seen as generic problems of social democracy), and second, that the rather stylized account of a 'crisis' of this system is taken to exhaust the historical experience of social democratic regimes in this period (with the presumption that alternative forms of social democratic politics did not and perhaps could not exist). A fairly casual review of the most familiar macro-economic indicators for the period since the mid-1970s makes it clear that any account which posits a 'common' fate for social democracy in the ensuing period is wide of the mark. Garrett (1998) is particularly effective in showing not just this diversity but also that the extent to which national regimes were social democratic was not a good indicator of their economic underperformance. (Indeed Garrett makes precisely the opposite case.) And yet, told often enough, these stories about the implausibility of social democratic strategies become sedimented as part of the common sense of politicians and policy-makers and help to define the limits not just of what can be done but also of what can be thought.

There is an alternative: the 'other' social democracies

Despite its enduring authority, this is not the only important account of social democratic politics in the recent period. Both in theory and in practice, there have been other ways of thinking about doing social democratic politics. At the theoretical level, and often quite explicitly in response to the perceived difficulties of the prevailing regimes, there have been a number of attempts to envisage alternative mechanisms through which what are still broadly social democratic ends could be realized. Western market socialists (see Nove, 1983; Miller, 1989; Roemer, 1994; C. Pierson, 1995), for example, propose a very radical and classically socialist move (towards the partial socialization of the ownership of the means of production), but this is seen as a way of delivering a set of characteristically social democratic ambitions (social citizenship plus a squeezed income profile in a context of representative democratic institutions). Similarly, the most articulate recent advocate of the move towards a Citizens' Basic Income presents this as a way of pursuing what are still desirable social democratic ambitions (securing social justice and economic efficiency under conditions of optimal individual liberty) in circumstances where these can no longer be delivered through the traditional mechanisms of Keynesian welfare states (van Parijs, 1992, pp. 215–40; 1995). Interestingly, both of these otherwise rather different alternatives to existing social democratic politics bring social ownership (but not, so they suppose, state ownership) back in. It is one of the (many) ironies of social democratic politics that while critics to its right have often focused on its embrace of state ownership and planning, this was most often a rhetorical device aimed more at 'traditional' supporters in both party and electorate. State ownership varied from case to case (and does not convincingly mark off social democracy from other forms of interventionist state). In its turn, centralized planning has generally been rather marginal to social democracy.[2]

Perhaps more consequential (at least in a survey of what social democracy *has* been) are alternative ways of modelling the strategic practices of social democratic movements. Here I consider just two such cases (among several others). The first is the power resources model, which came to be widely associated with Swedish experience. The second (and much more controversially treated here as an alternative social democratic form of governance) is the Australian model of social protection.

The power resources model

What marks the power resources model as definitively a social democratic account is its explanation of the ways and directions in which politics makes a difference. Its debt to a Kautskyan reading of Marx is fairly readily apparent. The power resources model offers an account built around the division between economic and political powers, often presented as a contrast between the determinations of markets and politics. In the economic sphere, the decisive power resource is control over (capital) assets, the mechanism for its exercise is the (wage labour) contract and its principal beneficiary is the capitalist class. In the political sphere, by contrast, power flows from the strength of numbers, mobilized through the democratic process (by political parties), and tends to favour 'numerically large collectivities', especially the organized working class. Institutionalized power struggles under advanced capitalism are best understood as a struggle between the logic of the market and the logic of politics, struggles that are 'likely to be reflected in the development of social citizenship and the welfare state' (Korpi, 1989, p. 312). The more successful the social democratic forces of the organized working class, the more entrenched and institutionalized will the welfare state become and the more marginalized will be the principle of allocation through the market (Korpi, 1989; Esping-Andersen, 1985, 1990; for a more sceptical view, see Schwartz, 2000b).

Following Esping-Andersen's influential usage (1990), this social democratic strategy is often presented as 'decommodifying', that is as protecting workers from what would otherwise be the impact of their participation in an unregulated labour market. An extensive welfare state – with generous replacement rates and near-universal coverage – is certainly an important part of this model. Just as consequential, though, are the measures taken to promote economic growth and full employment and the fostering of those corporatist institutions through which the interests of capital and labour (including the distribution of income) can be mediated. Famously, in the Swedish case, this practice was embedded in the structures of the 'Rehn–Meidner' model in which managerial authority and investment decisions were left in private hands, while Social Democratic governments pursued expansive macro-economic policies designed to support full employment, allied to a progressive taxation regime aimed at reducing overall economic inequality and fostering an extensive area of collective provision (and public sector employment). An 'active labour market policy' – encouraging the reallocation of labour and capital from less to more efficient enterprises – and a 'solidaristic' wages policy – allowing for the centralized nego-tiation of wages and the reduction of differentials – were seen as essential in generating a political economy which could simul-taneously deliver full employment, a compressed wages structure and low inflation.

At first sight, this is an account of social democratic politics which seems close to the Croslandite model, and for some commentators (including Crosland himself) Sweden's experience charts a classical 'middle way', in which the zero-sum games of class struggle (from a lingering attachment to which Crosland was keen to wean the British labour movement) give way to an extensive and redistributive state which can be used to moderate the outcomes of what remains a dynamic capitalist market econ-omy. For others on the left, this was a time-limited politics of compromise. On this account, by the 1970s the enhanced and entrenched strength of Sweden's social democratic forces had made it both possible and necessary to press forward towards a much more clearly socialist regime (based on the socialization of the investment function). For others, the changed situation was much more ambiguous – with the compromise increasingly un-stable but open to a resolution that might favour either labour or capital.

Clearly, the boldest version of the left's strategy – the move to introduce wage earners' funds which would enforce a gradual socialization of the Swedish economy – failed. There is rather less consensus about the nature and severity of the more general difficulties which Sweden's social democratic forces have con-fronted over the past decade. 'The crisis of the Swedish model' has become a staple topic of the post-social democracy literature, but the nature of that crisis is still widely contested. For neoliber-als, it has just taken rather longer for the world to catch up with the malpractices of Sweden's social democrats. For them, it is the standard vices of social democracy – high and progressive taxes, a generous welfare state, ill-disciplined labour markets and poor productivity – that have spelt the end of Sweden's social democratic ascendancy, ushering in an era of high unemployment and public indebtedness. For more sympathetic critics, the crucial changes are technological (unseating the commonality of interest which underpinned Sweden's astonishing labour solidarity), the product of globalization (opening up the real possibility of capital defection from the terms of the Swedish compromise), or geopolitical (alignment with the practices of other European Union states following Sweden's accession in 1995) (Ryner, 1998). Those who have focused on the changing logics of differing 'varieties of capitalism' have detected pressure within the coordinated market economies to move away from a 'centralized egalitarian' towards a 'flexibly co-ordinated' model (Soskice, 1999, p. 124). For others again, the problems are less the product of deep-seated structural change than of poor policy, mistimed macro-economic management or just plain bad luck (Garrett, 1998).

The Australian model

The claim that Australia furnishes a distinctive and social democratic model is contentious, not least among Australians themselves (see, for example, Beilharz, 1994; Wiseman, 1996). Despite having given the world its first labour administration (in Queensland in 1899) and its first national majority government (in 1910), for much of the twentieth century the Australian Labor Party's hold on federal power was intermittent (Castles, Gerritsen and Vowles, 1996). Australia's one rather exciting and eventful engagement with European-style social democracy, under Gough Whitlam in the early 1970s, ended rather catastrophically with the notorious dismissal of the Labor government by the Governor-General on 11 November 1975. In fact, the most extended period of ALP government came under Bob Hawke and Paul Keating between 1983 and 1996, at a time when most Northern and Western European social democratic parties were on the back foot. While this certainly focused attention on the ALP (and its governing fellow party in New Zealand), critics argued that the Hawke and Keating administrations were simply engaged in the pursuit of an Anglo-Saxon neoliberal agenda under another and more populist name (Maddox, 1989). Floating the Australian dollar, deregulating the domestic economy and sponsoring privatization were all seen as steps *away* from what little social democracy Australians had come to enjoy.

There is, however, an alternative view in which Australian experience is redescribed as the pursuit of broadly social democratic ambitions by radically different means. This is a position that has been most consistently advanced in a series of books and articles by Frank Castles (1985, 1988, 1994; Castles and Pierson, 1997). Australia has been widely misunderstood in the comparative literature, so Castles argues, because many commentators (mostly Europeans) have sought to apply criteria drawn from European experience to an evaluation of the Australian case. In fact, organized labour in Australia has always been quite strong and for much of this century enjoyed full or over-full (white, male) employment. Wages were, again by international standards, relatively high. Yet, finding that the Australian welfare state is comparatively small and almost all benefits means tested, that social citizenship is correspondingly underdeveloped and that federal government throughout much of the postwar period was dominated by a coalition of the right, many European commentators have been persuaded to classify Australia as a liberal or small market-oriented welfare state in which social democracy never really developed (Therborn, 1987; Esping-Andersen, 1990).

In fact, Australian welfare arrangements and their relation to the wider economy have always been quite different from those with which we are familiar in the most comparable advanced industrialized societies in Europe and North America. In particular, an unusual degree of social protection has been delivered through the occupational structure and much of Australia's 'welfare effort' is not captured by an exclusive focus on the conventional mechanisms of social security provision. Indeed, what is most distinctive about the Australian experience is that, from early in the century until at least the 1970s, most social protection was secured not through the state's social security apparatus but rather by regulation of a highly protectionist economy and, above all, through a mandatory and legally stipulated 'fair wages' policy. The combination of a 'fair wage', tight labour markets, protection for domestic industries and high levels of owner occupation made for a policy context quite different from that prevailing in Europe. In combination with a system that offered flat-rate and means-tested benefits funded out of general taxation, the Australian social security regime tended to be small but quite strongly redistributive.

By the turn of the 1980s this distinctive 'Australian settlement' within which social and economic life had been managed in the eighty years since Federation had begun to look increasingly vulnerable (see P. Kelly, 1992). Having been one of the world's most affluent countries for nearly a century, Australia had fallen back to lie somewhere in the middle of the OECD pack and by 1983 unemployment had risen to 10 per cent (Jones, 1996, pp. 10–11, 143). Unable to rely any longer on the remnants of the old trading relationship with Britain, with declining terms of trade and with little foreign investment in domestic manufacturing, the old regime of 'protection all around' looked increasingly dysfunctional (P. Kelly, 1992). It was in this context and under these pressures that the First Hawke–Keating administration embarked on a radical economic policy of financial deregulation. The dramatic centrepiece of this reform process was the flotation of the Australian dollar and the abolition of exchange controls in December 1983. In Kelly's account, 'the float transformed the economics and politics of Australia . . . It signalled the demise of the old Australia' (1992, p. 76). It was this financial deregulation, the later privatizations of Qantas and the Commonwealth Bank, and Hawke and Keating's high-profile friendships with Australia's new entrepreneurial buccaneers that helped to generate an image abroad (and, for some, at home) of the new Australian Labor Party (ALP) as a market-sympathetic or even neoliberal party.

The 'other side' of the Hawke–Keating regime, however, was a series of quasi-corporatist accords negotiated with the Australian Council of Trade Unions (ACTU), the central trade union organization which Hawke himself had led in the 1970s. The Accord process (which lasted in its various manifestations down to the defeat of the ALP in 1996) was originally designed to deliver a consensus for economic (and employment) growth without inflation through the unions' exercise of restraint in a context of highly centralized wage fixing. The Accord was not, however, just a mechanism for delivering wage restraint. Concessions in terms of wages were to be traded for a wider influence on government economic policy and improvements in the social wage.

In Castles's view (1994), the Hawke–Keating reforms represented not an abandonment but a 'refurbishment' of the Australian model. Certainly the domestic policy options of the ALP in government were severely constrained by the choice it made to reposition Australia in the regional and international economy. But within these limits, so Castles argues, it sought to reconcile the competing imperatives of public expenditure restraint, equity and benefit adequacy by a mixture of greater *targeting* alongside some benefit *enhancement*.

Perhaps the most problematic area of the reformed system lay in the tension between pursuing a policy of financial deregulation and maintaining a strongly regulated labour market. Since the established system had relied so heavily on legally set terms and conditions of employment as a surrogate for other forms of social provision, the erosion of the awards system (the quasi-judicial process under which statutory wage rates and working conditions are set) is liable to generate serious gaps in social protection. Labour market deregulation under the ALP was partial and incremental (for the contrast with New Zealand, see Kelsey, 1995), but decentralizing and simplifying the awards process presented severe difficulties in the closing years of the Keating government and the attempt to achieve improvements in productivity through greater enterprise bargaining tested to the limits the ALP–ACTU commitment to deregulation (Gruen and Grattan, 1993; P. Kelly, 1992).

These difficulties with labour market deregulation and the subsequent loss of two federal elections have persuaded some that, however distinctive the Australian model may have been, it is now a spent force. Others have concluded that the ALP did little more than slow a process of growing deregulation and inequality which more conservative forces subsequently took up with renewed zeal.[3] John Wiseman (1996) insists that the ALP's 'progressive competitiveness' turns out to be little more than 'a kinder road to hell'. Whatever one's verdict on the overall experience of these reforms, they do raise a number of interesting issues about alternative forms of social democratic governance. First, if we are concerned above all with resource *outcomes* rather than institutional *procedures*, they suggest that there may be alternative ways of squeezing income profiles (if more traditional social democratic processes prove either politically or economically 'too costly'). Secondly, they suggest that there may be ways of targeting resources which do not bear the stigma (and avoid the problems of perverse incentives and confiscatory effective marginal taxation rates) with which they are widely associated in Europe (though these possibilities may be context-specific). Thirdly, they are an interesting experiment in what may (and may not) be possible through state regulation of labour markets and social protection, and an illustration of the prospects for change in a comparatively small but highly redistributive welfare state. Finally, though, they also suggest the vulnerability of such a regime when faced by a government with a 'real' neoliberal agenda. The possible lessons of this Australian experience are something to which we return briefly in the final chapter.

Appraising social democracy

We are now in a position to draw some provisional conclusions from this extended but still highly selective journey through the history of social democracy. At its simplest, we can see that social democracy describes a diverse, long-standing and contested tradition. If we consider just the cases of Sweden, the UK and Australia, we find quite different 'operating conditions', and within these quite different constitutional, economic, geopolitical and social circumstances. While some commentators would make this the basis for a comparison of different social democratic experiences, others would insist that only one of these cases (Sweden, of course!) counts as 'truly' social democratic. In fact, social democratic experience is just too varied to be brought under a single and simple formulation. In itself, this is not an especially grave problem. In practice, though, the meaning of social democracy has been not so much contested as simply taken for granted. But these 'taken-for-granted' meanings vary enormously. One important body of research (from Michels to Kitschelt) treats social democracy as principally the name of a party and investigates it in terms of the dynamics of parties and party systems (Michels, 1949; Kitschelt, 1994). Others, such as Garrett

(1998), identify social democracy with a tightly specified model of a strong corporatist regime uniting labour party and centralized trade union organization (of which there are comparatively few examples, almost all confined to northern Europe). For others again, as in Giddens (1994, 1998), social democracy is a very expansive term which covers almost anything that is broadly 'left of centre'. Beyond this, there remains the suspicion that for some authors social democracy *really* means Sweden, with the possible addition of those systems that have sought more or less successfully to emulate it (Korpi, 1983). These several social democracies are also very much the product of particular times and places. No one could make sense of the disposition of Social Democrats in postwar continental Europe, or, indeed, of the 'new' Social Democrats of the recently democratized southern European states of the 1980s, without understanding the impact of fascism. It is perhaps better to recognize this diversity than to try to bring all these cases under some unifying umbrella. But given this, it is also clearly impossible to make generalizations about the overall plausibility of social democratic politics by considering the difficulties (or, indeed, the successes) of a particular state or even a number of states in a particular historical period.

This does not mean that we have simply to give up the search for any kind of coherence in the social democratic experience. In seeking out commonalities, we could argue, following Selucky (1979) echoing Keynes, that what unites all social democrats is the attempt to confront the problem of reconciling three things: 'economic efficiency, social justice and individual liberty'. This might seem like a neat solution, but since Keynes describes this as 'the political problem of mankind' it is not clear that it really helps to narrow our focus on a uniquely social democratic problematic. In fact, what most persuasively identifies social democratic politics is not so much particular policy instruments (however generally these are characterized), perhaps not even policy ambitions (beyond a very general disposition to ameliorate some types and levels of inequality), but rather an approach to the political process – above all, a commitment to piecemeal and 'progressive' change through legal-constitutional and generally parliamentary methods. Every now and then social democrats have thought a little more creatively about what democracy might mean and where it might happen. Occasionally, they have canvassed the possibility of quite radical reform through parliamentary procedures. But if anything, the social democratic commitment to an exclusively parliamentary form of democracy has become firmer with time.

Along with a belief in the capacity of parliamentary democracy to legislate social change has typically gone a faith in the capacity of the state bureaucracy and of the public sector more generally to deliver on these progressive policies. Bernstein and Kautsky both showed a keen awareness of the dangers of bureaucratization if too many powers passed into the hands of the central state and this fed their scepticism about the promise of public ownership. Levels of state ownership have varied widely, and certainly nationalization cannot be exclusively identified with parties of the left. Nonetheless, throughout the greater part of its history, social democracy has persisted in the belief that state institutions and civil servants – the tradition of 'public service' – were the appropriate means for delivering its agenda. Indeed, it was often this faith in the ethos of 'public service' rather than a concern with social ownership that fuelled the social democratic commitment to the public sector and helped to redeem its claim to be a politics of extended citizenship.

At the same time, social democratic politics has always been resolutely possibilist or pragmatic. Social democrats do have characteristic values – or at least sympathies – and historically they have pursued an agenda for 'social reform' which reflects these. But these ambitions are always mediated in practice by political circumstances. This is not to say that social democrats are unprincipled – or, at least, systematically more unprincipled than anyone else. It is to argue that social democratic judgements are always very strongly context-bound and that being available to fight on another day is almost always to be preferred to heroically taking the field against the odds. Since social democrats aim to use public policy and state power to effect incremental reforms – in circumstances where the principal levers of non-elected power are seen to lie in the hands of their opponents – and since ignoring social democratic reforms will often be enough to make them go away, they have had a more than usual concern for their electability.

Accommodation is the name of the social democratic game – and not only in those corporatist democracies which privilege the forging of consensus. Whether or not it is the appropriate lesson to draw, it is clear that the experience of the rise of fascism taught European social democrats that self-restraint may be the appropriate response to even quite predatory forms of liberal capitalism, just so long as the alternative is judged to be worse. A somewhat similar logic informs contemporary social democratic calls for 'socialism in one class' as a response to the widening income inequality generated by a more assertive globalized capitalism (Scharpf, 1991). In part, this is just a restatement of the structural dependency thesis: that social democratic governments committed to legal-constitutional methods and economic growth must attend to the interests of mobile capital, even when these clash with what appear to be the immediate needs of social democracy's principal electoral constituency. But there is also a lingering political concern (with some good historical precedents) that a labour movement which can frighten but not deliver is liable to find its gains eroded by populist politicians of the right. (This may be seen as the lesson not only of fascism but also, for example, of Britain in the 1970s.) In the end, this shades over into the argument that it is better for social democratic forces to give capital what it wants than to have the same goods delivered by a party of the right. The problem with *this* logic is that it appears to give licence to 'social democratic' politicians to pursue almost any political agenda, however damaging to the interests of its supporters, on the grounds that the alternative (right-wing policies delivered by right-wing parties) would be worse. Judging the extent to which the hands of reluctant social democratic politicians were forced by circumstances beyond their control is a fine art.

If the meaning of 'democracy' in social democracy is reasonably clear and fairly conventional, 'social' has at some time been taken to mean almost everything from the complete socialization of ownership of the means of production and exchange to the most mild-mannered and inconsequential of incremental reforms. An intellectual history of social democracy is bound to give pride of place to revisionism since this yields both the most sustained defence of its principles and the most coherent account of its emergence. But this is almost certainly to overestimate the specifically socialist element in the social democratic tradition. It is not that socialist thinking is not an important component of social democracy. Indeed, its rather hazy identification with socialist ideas alongside some sort of an institutional linkage with trade unions has helped social democratic parties to be the most successful mobilizers of working-class votes. But, in fact, social democracy is as much marked by other forms of 'progressive' thought, above all by that social liberalism from which it is not easily distinguished. Socialism – often understood above all in distributional terms – takes its place alongside a concern for the poor, the nation, economic and administrative efficiency, modernization and social justice as characteristic themes of social democratic politics. Certainly, that shorthand which variously describes social democracy as 'socialism plus democracy' or 'the ideology of socialism plus parliamentary democracy' or, less flatteringly, as 'parliamentary cretinism masked by socialist rhetoric' proves quite inadequate to historical experience.

It is perhaps this broader base in 'progressive' opinion plus an overriding concern with electability which has drawn social democrats to speak so frequently in the language of citizenship. And where this language of citizenship has seemed too hard-edged or assertive, too much grounded in the language of rights, there has been some movement to invoke 'community' as a rather more amorphous alternative. The move from workers' parties to peoples' parties and from workers to citizens is, of course, in part driven by an electoral logic. (At its simplest, there are just not enough workers' votes to underwrite stable social democratic majorities.) But it also accords with a wider social democratic sentiment, that in so far as social democrats aspire to socialism it is (to paraphrase Bernstein) in order to forge a socialist democracy and not a proletarian one. Of course, the nature of citizenship (including social citizenship) or 'community' is itself far from straightforward and, among its critics, as much associated now with exclusion as inclusion. Classical social democratic settlements were (sometimes quite explicitly) racist and certainly strongly gendered. If social democratic citizenship – and its welfare regime – were built around work, this was, as Pateman (1988) has argued, largely the waged employment of a predominantly male workforce in formal labour markets. But here, as elsewhere, one must exercise some caution. Social democratic regimes have varied considerably in terms of their outcomes for women and people from differing ethnic minorities.

Having directed attention away from a substantive social democratic agenda, it is nonetheless clear that, historically, social democrats have been identified with both particular issues and policies. Given social democracy's varying forms of association with organized labour, typical workers' concerns – health and safety, insurance against loss of income, rights of collective organ-ization – have always been high on the agenda. Similarly, employ-ment and unemployment were abiding concerns for social democrats in both pre- and postwar years (as they are now). Of course, the aspiration to achieve full employment was rarely expressed on behalf of all citizens. But, undoubtedly, full (male) waged employment was seen as desirable in itself and also as essential in making a 'generous' and social democratic welfare state 'affordable'. The rather more modest contemporary ambition of 'maximizing employability' is invested with many of the same virtues. Also retraceable to the 1930s, though a little less prominent, is a concern with uneven development. In Britain, 'the problem' was 'the North', in Italy it was 'the South'. But regional inequality as much as class inequality (though obviously the two were not independent) was a continuing concern for social democrats. Social democrats, with their key electoral con-stituency among those least favoured by prevailing markets for capital and labour, consistently supported public services on the basis that an administrative or 'needs' basis for the allocation of goods and services was likely to optimize outcomes for their natural supporters. In time, of course, the providers as well as the recipients of public services became a key constituency of support for Social Democratic parties.

In practice, welfare states, even those that have been subclas-sified as social democratic, have varied significantly in size, struc-ture and intent and we need to attend to these important differences if we are to avoid the trap of generalizing, as some have been tempted to do, about the past and present of 'the social democratic welfare state'. Certainly, any straightforward suggestion that social democratic regimes were unseated by a unique propensity to 'tax and spend' sits a little uneasily with the history of taxation and with the comparative history of welfare states themselves. We need to be a little cautious too about the supposition that social democracy was uniquely committed to Keynesian demand management. Again, experience was quite varied and social democrats used a range of tools to achieve (or fail to achieve) their economic goals. It was not always the 'most' social democratic states that ran the largest budget deficits. (On these qualifications, see Garrett, 1998, 2000.) Levels of formal public ownership also varied widely. 'Planning' (as part of a 'planned economy') was extremely limited and often came in practice to mean incomes policies plus demand management (Ellman, 1989).There was certainly a presumption in favour of a mixed economy, governmental responsibility for maximizing employment and a commitment to divert increasing resources into a publicly administered social wage. There was a widespread belief that it was a legitimate (but not the sole) function of progressive taxation regimes to narrow inequalities of income and opportunity. But the extent to which these ambitions were embodied in policy varied widely across time and between states and parties.

Most consequentially, in terms of the arguments to follow, social democracy cannot be reduced to the Keynesian welfare state, even where this is cashed out as something more than a few headline principles. It would be foolish to deny that the idea of the KWS captures something about the experience of social democratic politics and its difficulties over the past fifty years. It sometimes seems as if it is the commitment to some sort of 'collective' welfare provision that most plausibly distinguishes social democrats from left-leaning liberals. But close up, the KWS turns out to have meant rather different things in different places. Its 'crisis' proves to have been hardly less variable. Social democrats have never accepted that the cumulative outcomes of market exchanges are just or equitable or liberty-maximizing or (necessarily) efficient. But, historically, they did arrive at the judgement (1) that markets are more efficient than any other alternative and defensible because they can be manipulated by governments, or (2) that the costs of the alternatives to private property and markets are too great (either economically or in terms of some other valued good, such as individual liberty), or (3) that although we would be better off without markets (or markets based on the existing distributions of economic assets), the costs of transition would outweigh the benefits. They have generally subscribed to something which, at its fanciest, is called a politics of social citizenship – in which political power and resources are to be used to countermand the actions of markets to the extent necessary to ensure that all members of a political community are able to operationalize (with equal effect or at least above some acceptable minimum) certain rights and capacities *as citizens*. Less grandly, social democratic politics has been about checking the outcomes of markets in the interest of those who are disadvantaged but representable. (Social democracy has characteristically defended most effectively the interests of those who are individually weak but organizable. The citizenship of those who fail to make it into labour markets – the powerless – has never been quite so crucial.)

Finally, social democrats have generally been committed to achieving economic growth – and it is probably legitimate to argue that elements of their particular growth regime came to be counterproductive both politically and perhaps economically (see Kitschelt, 1994). Of course, this commitment to economic growth is an aspect of modern politics that goes far beyond social democracy. In practice, neoliberal opponents generated much more political capital by claiming that social democracy was inimical to growth than from their insistence that social democracy was the enemy of individual liberty. If (as Giddens among others imagines) a key contemporary issue is 'the politics of less' – of how to slow that juggernaut which ties economic growth to environmental degradation, while also addressing the growing global inequalities of incomes and resources – this is an issue which challenges, but also reaches far beyond, social democracy. On the other hand, social democracy offers almost our only successful experience of negotiated decrementalism plus social protection.

Conclusion

In these opening chapters I have tried to establish something of the range and diversity of the social democratic tradition. Above all, I have tried to show that accounts like those of Gray and Giddens which identify social democracy with a particular time, place and institutional form are mistaken. The theoretical, institutional and electoral roots of modern social democracy are more complex and diverse than these accounts suggest. Similarly, the difficulties that social democrats have faced and the solutions they have fashioned are more variable and, in some instances, more successful than Gray and Giddens seem to suppose. Accordingly, I would suggest that those reconstructions of the social democratic past which require us to see it as having no future need to be challenged. But we have still to deal with the belief that, however its past may be reassessed, the real obstacle to a future social democratic politics lies in quite new challenges for which it is (perhaps uniquely) ill-suited. The two key challenges here are globalization and demographic change. Before we turn to an assessment of what futures remain open, we need to consider these two strategic challenges.

4

Globalization and the End of Social Democracy

The 'third way' is only the most recent and prominent expression of a more general disposition over the past fifteen years to reassess the premises of a contemporary social democratic politics.[1] In general, there has been a supposition that the 'old' ways of doing social democratic politics, above all through a politics of redistribution managed by a centralized state, are no longer viable (and, indeed, on several accounts, no longer desirable). A number of economic and political changes are seen to mandate the search for a new political machinery of social amelioration. Two such sets of changes have particular prominence in recent accounts: processes of globalization and demographic change. In this chapter, I focus on the first of these challenges. At its simplest, a more 'traditional' social democracy is seen to have built its politics of social amelioration on stable political constituencies within clearly demarcated national economies managed by efficacious centralized states in a broadly bipolar world order. Globalization has removed all these certainties and with them both the constituency and the modalities of a social democratic politics. For some, this really does look like the end of the line. According to John Gray, 'social democracy has been removed from the agenda of history' (1998, p. 99). In what follows, I subject this account to critical scrutiny in three key areas: trade, capital mobility and the changing international division of labour.

What is globalization?

While there is no universal agreement about precisely what globalization connotes, by now the broad *domain* of globalization is not hard to establish. At its simplest, it refers to 'the widening, deepening and speeding up of worldwide interconnectedness' (Held et al., 1999, p. 2). On this account, globalization has four interrelated dimensions:

1   *Extensity*: increasing scope or 'stretching' of social, political and economic activities across frontiers.
2   *Intensity*: an intensification of these interconnections in frequency and significance.
3   *Velocity*: a speeding up of these global interactions (and reactions).
4   *Impact*: an 'enmeshment' of differing 'locales', so that 'global' events have an increasing salience for local, national and regional communities. (Held et al., 1999, pp. 15–16)

The numbers on which the case for the transformative importance of globalization is built are disarmingly simple and yet mind-boggling. World trade in goods has grown almost twice as fast as GDP since 1950. The trade in services also appears to have doubled in the period since figures were first reported in 1980, so that total world trade may now amount to as much as 45 per cent of world GDP. Although much of this trade takes place *within* the developed world or, even more narrowly, within its three key regional economies, there is some evidence of rising trade between developed and developing economies (although much of this growth has been focused on South East Asia). There are also signs of growth in trade in manufactured goods and of increasing intra-industry trading *within* the developed economies. At the same time, the technologies of transportation and, above all, of communication have been transformed and the associated costs have fallen substantially. Containerization significantly reduced the costs of long-distance sea transport in the postwar world (by up to two-thirds). International telephone traffic is rising by about 20 per cent per year (from around 67.5 billion minutes in 1996), and the canny caller can now make an intercontinental call for a fraction of what it would have cost even a decade ago (when prices had already fallen steeply). The costs of computing technology have similarly continued to fall and, within the last decade, the internet has emerged as a form of 'mass' communication (if still for comparatively few) throughout the developed world. The number of international tourists rose from about 25 million with an expenditure of about $2 billion in 1950 to over half a billion in 1995 with an annual spend of $255 billion, taking unprecedented numbers of human beings around the globe. (See Held et al., 1999; Garrett, 1999.)

A crucial part in the story of economic globalization is taken by the growth in the numbers and influence of multinational corporations (MNCs) and rising foreign direct investment (FDI). In 1998, 53,000 MNCs had global sales of $9.5 trillion, accounting for about a quarter of world output and up to 70 per cent of world trade. The hundred largest MNCs had 6 million employees worldwide and accounted for about 20 per cent of global foreign assets. Though still disproportionately based in the US, MNCs can now be found across much of the world economy and, while once they were focused largely on primary goods and manufacturing, there is now a very significant level of multinational activity in the service sector. Alongside this growth in MNCs there has been a rapid rise in foreign direct investment, which grew fivefold between 1980 and 1994 to stand at around $250 billion. In the 1980s and 1990s, most developed states saw an increase in both inward *and* outward FDI and this has contributed to a growing engagement of national economies with the global order (Held et al., 1999, pp. 259–82).

Still more dramatic are those figures that disclose a transformation in patterns of financial activity around the globe. In a context of twenty-four hour trading and more or less instantaneous electronic transmission of data, turnover in foreign exchange markets rose from $17.5 trillion in 1979 to over $300 trillion in the late 1990s. Only a small part of this increase has been devoted to servicing the rapid growth in world trade (with the ratio of foreign exchange turnover to trade standing at around 60:1). A good deal of this trading represents speculative activity. With the combined reserves of all the world's central banks representing no more than a single day's trading volume, sustained movements against particular currencies triggered a succession of spectacular devaluation crises through the 1990s. The period since the mid-1980s has also seen the dramatic rise of trading in various financial derivatives (futures, options, swaps), growth in international bank lending and in the issuing of international bonds. Governments now find that an increasing proportion of their debt is held by foreign investors and domestic stock exchanges have seen a near-tripling in the foreign ownership of equities. Of course, capital flows in themselves may not give a clear measure of capital mobility. After all, in neoliberal heaven, all the capital would be efficiently allocated and movements would be zero! But a simple index of government restrictions on international capital flows shows these to have fallen steadily since 1973 (generating a corresponding rise in capital mobility) and, while there is no evidence of the emergence of a single 'world' interest rate (implying the frictionless mobility of capital), there are signs that long-term rates are converging and that, at the very least, 'national interest rates are determined in the context of global financial markets and conditions' (Garrett, 1998, p. 56; Held et al., 1999, pp. 206–9, 216, 219).

The third crucial element in this part of the globalization story is the transformation in the international (and often consequently the domestic) division of labour. This is clearly a central feature in John Gray's account of the demise of social democracy, and industrial relocation, especially of manufacturing capacity, has been an important part of the anecdotal history of globalization at least since the 1960s. In part, this just reflects the enormous growth in MNCs and their economic activity. Global production networks, the 'world car' and global brands are all aspects of the growing intensity and extensity of global economic relationships generated by rising FDI and multinational activity. But there is also a more general trend towards the relocation of particular types of industrial activity and, with it, employment. In its classical form, this account holds that (at least since the 1960s) there has been a tendency for manufacturing production to relocate away from 'the North' or the most advanced industrial states towards a succession of newly industrialized economies (NIEs) or 'the South' (though the latter is hardly an apt term given the extent to which this migration of production has largely bypassed Africa and focused on South East Asia) (Froebel, Heinrichs and Kreile, 1980).

A number of changes have driven this move: (1) a flow of migrants into cities in less developed countries, producing a large pool of cheap labour, in a context where either (2) production processes rely on unskilled labour, or (3) existing levels of educational attainment are quite high, and (4) collapsing transportation and communication costs make production at sites remote from the point of consumption economically viable. Typically starting with textiles and steel manufacture, a number of industries have migrated from developed to developing economies, creating a situation in which the less developed countries no longer simply export raw materials but also increasingly export manufactured goods which can now compete on world markets. The share of world exports of manufactured goods taken by developing countries (excluding China) doubled between 1980 and 1995 (Held et al., 1999, p. 173).

These changes in the location of production have an impact on patterns of employment within the developed economies (with the most extensive welfare states). In particular, there is a decline in the demand for unskilled labour and a growing premium for marketable skills. This is seen to feed a tendency for both growing unemployment among the unskilled and/or a greater dispersion in wages between the skilled and the unskilled. There is also a suggestion that, without some form of institutional intermediation, this will also tend to generate a greater diversity in the dynamics through which wages are set in the traded and non-traded sectors of the economy.

Social democracy and the 'imperatives' of globalization

At first sight, the evidence that globalization constitutes something qualitatively and quantitatively new appears powerful, but it still remains to be explained how these changes are supposed to spell the end of traditional social democratic politics. First, we need to observe that for most of its critics (and many of its allies) social democracy is more or less identified with the Keynesian welfare state or with Crosland's slightly more cumbersome 'Keynes-plus-modified-capitalism-plus-Welfare-State'. For others, it is best embodied in the distinctive institutional arrangements of democratic corporatism. Above all, it is seen to have been based on *national* settlements in which governments use the strength of *organized numbers* (essentially the powers of trade unions or unions allied to social democratic parties) and *state power* to tie capital in to arrangements (and costs) which it would otherwise seek to avoid. Social democracy is seen to depend on partially autonomous national economies (though located within a supportive international environment) with room, within limits, for effective government control and with the capacity to resource and deliver an extensive system of social protection. It is in the context of social democracy understood in these terms that globalization poses such a challenge. In essence, globalization increases the porosity of international borders, heightens the mobility of capital, disorganizes the internal homogeneity of the 'labour interest' and correspondingly disempowers the social democratic form of the interventionist state. Here I consider this argument in a little more detail in each of the three key areas I have identified – trade, capital mobility and a changing division of labour.

Trade

On this account, the rise in trade is crucial in undermining the autonomy of what can no longer be properly described as domestic economies. Although the major developed economies were clearly never autarchic (though some were much more exposed to international trends than others), they are now more than ever involved in trade (both importing and exporting). Firms must compete in international marketplaces and that means with those rivals who are best able to contain costs in producing goods and services of similar quality. This introduces the favourite political mantra of the 1990s: 'competitiveness'. In order to survive in a world of increasing trade, nations, their enterprises and their workers (frequently and rather carelessly conflated) must be able to compete.

Corporations may seek to compete in terms of either quality or cost and they may seek to control costs either through raising productivity or reducing the price of inputs. Overall, they are bound to be concerned with processes of cost containment. In developed social democratic states, so it is argued, costs tend to be high: salaries and employment are protected by corporatist institutions, legal minima and an extensive social wage. To fund this, taxes and non-wage labour costs also need to be high. But firms in these states have now to compete in international markets with producers with lower wages, a much more rudimentary social security infrastructure and more primitive labour legislation. Some have argued that this is enough to draw social democratic states into a nightmarish 'race to the bottom' in terms of social provision and wages. More commonly, and a little more soberly, it is argued that developed states, with comparatively high wages and an extensive social infrastructure, can only avoid being drawn into such a struggle by evolving quite new countervailing strategies. In the new and open trading order, they can (only) compete and sustain standards of living by moving from a 'passive' (or rights-based) to a more 'active' (and employment-oriented) welfare state, by 'flexibilizing' labour markets and allowing for greater wage dispersal (while seeking to foster a skills economy), by reforming their tax systems (to make them less progressive and to redistribute costs away from capital and the employment of labour), and 'rationalizing' public sector services (to increase their 'efficiency'). Societies must become 'active' and economies 'competitive'. Governments may reform by being 'clever' rather than scything through their systems of social protection, but in the process they are bound to establish regimes which are quite different from those classically identified with social democracy.

Capital mobility

The contours of the argument from the heightened mobility of capital are a little different, though the presumed consequences turn out to be much the same. In essence, the argument is that the enhanced mobility of capital – and the superenhanced mobility of financial capital – have disempowered national governments or, at the very least, that they have transformed the parameters within which such governments work, so that the interests of financial asset-holders will always trump those of anyone else (including the political community as a whole). This may be presented as one more version of the argument for the *structural dependence* of governments on business: that governments in liberal democratic societies are in the last instance reliant for resources on the willingness of the holders of private financial assets to invest (see Lindblom, 1977; Przeworski and Wallerstein, 1988). Whatever their political ambitions or their constituency, so it is argued, governments find themselves obliged first and foremost to service the interests of (big) business. With the growing internationalization of capital, governments have to consider the perceived interests and expectations of internationally diverse investors. The expectation is that internationally mobile capital will be seeking out the highest and the swiftest (secure) returns and the lowest cost environment. Even the implicit threat of 'exit' by mobile capital may be enough to make governments respond pre-emptively to what they perceive the interests of these asset-holders to be. Governments will compete with each other, it is suggested, to offer the most favourable terms for inward investment and those with resources to invest and plants to build will find themselves in a position to extract favourable terms from a series of competing suitors.

The changing division of labour

Finally, changes in both the international and domestic division of labour, allied to the above reorientation of government policy, alter the patterns of support on which the traditional social democratic state was constructed. Social democracy both built on and helped to constitute the commonality of interest of waged workers or the carefully crafted alliance of interests between working and middle classes. But growing trade and a division of labour founded at the international rather than the domestic level mean that the interests of workers (especially as between those in the traded and non-traded sectors of the economy) diverge. To some extent these interests have always diverged and centralized trade union institutions existed to manage and contain these divergences. But it becomes increasingly difficult to sustain solidarity across these divisions if trade unions become less effective or levels of union density decline or if capital just becomes less interested in participating in corporatist institutions (because it no longer needs the compliance which these arrangements were thought to deliver). Thus the business of acting collectively in the labour interest becomes more difficult as the real immediate interests of workers in different sectors diverge, while, at the very same time, the institutions which helped to promote and coordinate their common interests are weakened. This problem is made still more acute where a key power resource of labour – full employment – has been lost. In this way, changes in the global economy not only have a direct impact on social democracy's governing capacity, they also tend to disorganize its power base and to deplete its political resources.

The real impact of globalization

It is surely concerns of this kind that underpin the call for a 'renewal' of social democracy or a 'third way'. Some make a virtue of the new order by pointing to the (often quite genuine) vices of the 'old' social democracy (its gendered settlement and its insensitivity to individual needs, though not, of course, its failure to deliver real change). Others, with a classically pragmatic approach, seek out the least damaging way of dealing with a new era of social decrementalism. Capital has won and the duty of social democrats is to salvage what they can and to protect those who are least able to protect themselves in the brave new world. Underpinning all of this is a sense that globalization has indeed undermined the premises on which classical social democratic politics was built, mandating that something else must take its place.

But before we endorse this judgement, we should pause to consider the evidence a little more closely. Some commentators remain profoundly sceptical about the claims that globalization is either very new or especially newly efficacious. To cite a popular example, critics insist that heightened levels of world trade now are simply a *return* to the sorts of levels that prevailed in the period before 1914 (Hirst and Thompson, 1996; Held et al., 1999). Similarly, Colin Hay (1999) is insistent that the imagined consequences of globalization far outstrip its 'real' impact and that much of the ground conceded by social democrats has been given up unnecessarily (or for other reasons). It is certainly timely to be reminded that the process of globalization is indeed nothing new and that ideas (including very bad ones) can (through however obscure a process) become a real material force (Hall, 1989). My argument here, however, is not that nothing (much) has changed. While not unprecedented, many of the changes identified with globalization do indeed seem to me to constitute something new in the character of the international order, yielding a qualitatively different order of international 'enmeshment' (Held et al., 1999). I am much more concerned to establish whether these changes actually warrant the kinds of judgements that have been made about the continuing relevance or viability of older forms of social democracy. The evidence for this seems to me to be much less certain.

The impact of trade

We now have considerable and detailed data with which to assess the claims made about the impact of globalization and, as we shall see, the record is rather patchy. Certainly I think we have to reject the claim that trade openness in and of itself is inimical to social democratic state practices – the view that states or, at least, successful states in an open trading environment will tend to be low in taxation and low in social provision. Katzenstein (1985) was one of the first to draw attention to the fact that several of the smaller and most open economies of northern Europe were also those with the largest public budgets and the most extensive social democratic institutions (in both welfare state and labour markets). A few years earlier, Cameron's (1978) survey had found that those countries with the most open trading economies had the largest public sectors and often the most strongly coordinated labour market institutions. These were societies which were generally successful in terms of a range of economic indicators (growth, employment and, though to a lesser degree, inflation). A widely canvassed explanation is that it was precisely the greater vulnerability to external shocks that led political forces in these states to construct an elaborate network of compensations (in welfare or public sector employment) for those who were disadvantaged by the open trading regime. From the general gains that trade afforded came the means to compensate those individuals and communities who were disadvantaged by it.

It might be argued that this association is time-limited by (what was then) the lower mobility of capital. Rodrik (1997), for example, argues that while openness may once have put upward pressure on public expenditure, as trade expands alongside heightened capital mobility this pressure may have been reversed. By contrast, Garrett (1998) maintains that even with the intensification of globalization there are still good reasons to think that an extensive public economy can be maintained. In part, this is because much of government spending is an investment, enhancing productivity and securing collective goods that are undersupplied by the market (including education, training and the development of physical and communications infrastructure). But Garrett wishes to extend this argument to apply to what are generally seen as 'non-productive' elements in social expenditure – including moderately generous transfers to the old, the sick and the disabled. In essence, his case is that these forms of provision, and the containment of income inequalities, will be attractive to even the most footloose of mobile capital because they underpin the 'intangible' but real benefits of social security, the social cohesion and trust which, in turn, make for high productivity. The counterfactual here is a state with low wages and levels of social expenditure but high levels of criminality, insecure property rights and heightened levels of social disorder. Businesses, particularly in capital-intensive manufacturing, will not seek out the lowest (social) cost environment, but those locations which will best guarantee their medium-term profitability. At the same time, globalization does increase the numbers of citizens who are economically insecure or vulnerable and, in this context, Garrett, in the face of most orthodox opinion, sees a potentially *growing* constituency for big government and left-of-centre parties (1998, pp. 10–11).

This democratic corporatist regime consists of four key elements:

> First, leftist governments enact economic policies that redistribute wealth and risk in ways that favor the increasingly large segments of the population that are vulnerable to the vicissitudes of global markets. Second, some of these policies are directly conducive to better economic performance because they promote collective goods that are undersupplied by the market (e.g. investments in

human capital and infrastructure). Third, the leaders of encom-
passing labor market institutions ensure that workers do not take
advantage of market-cushioning policies to act in ways that harm
the macroeconomy – most importantly, by gearing economywide
wage developments to the competitiveness of the sector of the
economy exposed to global markets. Finally, the political, economic, and social stability characteristics of social democratic corporatism – coupled with the high productivity of labor – provide
an attractive home for investors in the uncertain and volatile
international economy. (Garrett, 1998, p. 130)

Of course, this 'virtuous' response to the pressures of globalization should not be expected everywhere (and it is seen as only
one among many potential responses to capital market integration), but Garrett does insist that it is not just still viable, but
perhaps even exportable (1998, pp. 155–6).

The evidence that would give weight to Garrett's argument is
a little ambiguous, especially for the period after 1990. Indeed,
Garrett himself finds that in the most recent period those
countries in which trade has expanded most rapidly have seen
lower than average increases in the growth of government
expenditure. In the same period, trade seems to have constrained
budgets everywhere and there has been some convergence in
expenditure trends (though from very different starting points, so
that differences across states remain very substantial). But this
does not furnish unqualified support for that story which sees
jobs in the developed world being transferred to less developed
economies. Despite some changes in the global distribution of
trade, it remains the case that most of this increase lies *between*
the developed economies, rather than between these economies
and those in the developing world (Rodrik, 1997, p. 26; Held et
al., 1999, pp. 171–2). This may still, of course, place pressure on
domestic governments (and increase insecurity among workers)
but that is not quite the same as saying that it is competition
with the low-wage, low-social protection sectors of the world
economy that is undermining the integrity of interventionist
states in the advanced capitalist economies. At the same time, it
is just not clear that those developed societies with the most
extensive welfare states have actually fared any worse economically than comparable societies with a much smaller apparatus
of social protection (Pfaller, Gough and Therborn, 1991).

Meanwhile, the very logic of arguing from or for 'competitiveness' has been called into doubt. As Rodrik has it, 'policymakers often fall into the trap of using "competitiveness" as an excuse for needed domestic reforms [but] the term "competitiveness" itself is largely meaningless when applied to whole economies, unless it is used to refer to things that already have a proper name – such as productivity, investment, and economic growth' (1997, p. 79). In a similar vein, Paul Krugman (1994) insists that competitiveness has become a 'dangerous obsession'. It is apparently simple and graphic – both qualities which will recommend it to politicians and businesspeople – but its uses are either spurious (as in the phrase 'making the UK economy more competitive') or else empirically insignificant (as an explanation of European unemployment, for example). There certainly is some evidence that the greater substitutability of low-skilled labour across borders has an effect on unskilled workers and their wages in the developed economies – and that there may be a knock-on effect in terms of the incidence of non-wage costs (increasingly falling to labour), in the volatility of hours worked and wages earned, and in the incidence and effectiveness of labour unions (Rodrik, 1997, pp. 16–25). These changes are then in their turn likely to have an impact on the power resources of social democratic governments. But these may still not be the most important causes of income dispersion and unemployment, with most economists agreeing that technological change plays a much larger role than trade (Cline, 1997). Certainly, it is not the same as saying that 'competitiveness' is driving all societies and economies towards a residual, minimalist, liberal model for labour market governance and social protection (on the latter, see also Soskice, 1999).

The impact of capital mobility

Increased capital mobility, as we have seen, is widely supposed to have had the same sorts of political consequences as trade openness and these tendencies should become still more pronounced when, as is increasingly the case, the two coincide. Again, social democracy is said to be most vulnerable to increasing capital mobility because it is the governing form which is most reliant on intervention and redistribution and because it is associated with the largest public economies. Few critics dispute that there has been a real process of increasing mobility of finance capital over the past twenty years (evidenced above). They do, however, insist that both the level of integration of financial markets and its consequences have been exaggerated. In fact, markets for differing types of financial instruments are not fully integrated and, despite the increase in holdings of cross-border equities, there is continuing evidence of a domestic 'bias' in shareholdings and borrowing (Fligstein, 1998, pp. 28–9). Indeed, if global financial markets were really as integrated as some of the hyperglobalists believe, we would be deprived of one of the great spectacles of the global economy – the repeated feeding frenzies of speculation against vulnerable currencies. As with trade, much of the speculation in global financial markets is concentrated on the major currencies, notwithstanding the recurrent crises of a number of 'second-rank' currencies. Indeed, one of the signal features of globalization of both trade and capital is the extent to which significant areas of the world – sub-Saharan Africa, the Middle East and, to some extent, Latin America – have become *more* excluded from international economic processes in the most recent period. And, even in the age of instantaneous international transmissibility and twenty-four hour trading, the movement of capital around the globe is still not quite costless. After all, somebody has to pay the salaries of all those smart currency dealers.

There are other reasons to doubt whether the rise of a global capital market has had quite the political consequences reported for it. It has been widely argued that, given the heightened mobility of finance capital, governments would have increasing difficulty in raising revenue, or, at least, that there would be a transfer of taxation activity from capital towards labour, consumption or land. There would be a convergence towards low-tax, low-expenditure states. Large-scale reductions in social expenditure – widely anticipated since the first oil crisis in 1973 – have been a very long time coming. States have been variously 'reinvented', 'agencified' and 'privatized' but levels of public spending have still tended to creep upwards. Patterns are complex and, revealingly given some of the expectations about convergence, there continue to be very widespread differences between absolute levels of public expenditure even in the more developed states. Growth in the size of the public sector has just about been contained and certainly, given the demand for public services particularly among ageing populations, this can be seen as a reduction in the level of social protection. The bald fact, though, is that we still live in an epoch of big government (OECD, 1996, p. 15; 1998, pp. 157–67).

If we look at the way in which this big government is funded, we find that while there are changes they are not always those that the globalization story would lead us to expect. In a survey of seventeen developed states, Swank (1998b, p. 679) finds little evidence of changes in the levels of corporate taxation (as a percentage of operating income) between the 1970s and the 1990s. Any reductions in levels of taxation he finds to have been offset by the elimination of special incentives and allowances which government had previously allowed to corporations. This is in line, so Swank argues, with a significant change in government policies, which have switched from being market regulating or market shaping towards being more market conforming. Indeed, one of the aspirations of reforming administrations has been to prevent their revenue-raising behaviour from 'distorting' economic behaviour. Certainly tax reform can be seen to have been one element in a widespread growth in income inequality in the 1980s and 1990s as states have sought to 'flatten' their tax regimes. But governments have not for the most part been willing to see a significant decline in their overall tax take, and tax reforms of the 1980s and 1990s tended to be revenue neutral and more about broadening the base or redistributing the burden than cutting the overall level of taxes.

Of course, there may be other changes attendant on globalization which affect taxation of the corporate sector. Historically, it has always been easier to tax relatively immobile assets and, in addition to the heightened mobility of finance capital, increased multinational activity and transfer pricing may have made it much easier for firms to prevent their economic activity from being fully captured by revenue-raising authorities. The secular shift towards indirect consumption taxes may issue from the fact that they are both harder to avoid but at the same time less apparent to the taxpayer. Overall, there have been important changes in tax regimes over the past twenty years and many of these have moved in the direction that globalizers might anticipate. But it would still be a mistake to attribute all of these, at least directly, to the impact of globalization, not least because we need always to remember the tremendous 'pull' exercised on national taxation by a volatile mixture of demographic change, rising health-care costs and mass unemployment.

Social democratic states have always been seen as peculiarly vulnerable to a tightening of financial disciplines because it is they who are perceived to be most likely to run substantial budget deficits and/or to permit higher levels of inflation (although not perhaps, as in the US under Reagan, to initiate massive reflationary hikes in the defence budget). These are the policy dispositions which it is thought international asset-holders are most likely to want to punish. This may not express itself directly as capital flight but rather as a bidding down of the value of the deficit country's currency (in the expectation of future inflation) and the imposition of a premium on the interest rates of the offending government. Swank's results on this issue are interesting:

> Exposure to international capital markets . . . does not necessitate significant retrenchment of the welfare state at moderate levels of budget imbalance; when budget deficits don't exist, some expansion of social protection is possible even in the context of international capital mobility. *However, when budget deficits become high, capital mobility engenders cuts in social welfare effort.* (1998b)

Garrett's survey (1998, p. 19) suggests that social democratic corporatist states saw an above average rise in public indebtedness through the 1980s and a lower than average fall in inflation through the same period. He also finds evidence that interest rates were generally higher in these regimes as markets exacted a premium for their greater indebtedness. As he concludes, 'the left and organized labor had to pay a price for redistributive big government in the global economy' (p. 103).

All of this lends weight to the judgement of Perraton and his collaborators (2000, p. 295): 'rather than global financial markets imposing particular policies on national governments, they have significantly changed the costs associated with particular policies and instruments through their effects on interest rate risk premia and exchange rate movements.' At times, this may constitute an effective veto, with some economic options rendered 'prohibitively expensive', and it will certainly push governments 'to pursue national macroeconomic strategies which seek low and stable rates of inflation, through fiscal discipline and a tight monetary policy'. Thus an incoming social democratic government committed to a fixed inflation target may find it possible to maintain lower interest rates (and to encourage growth) by allowing autonomy to its central bank, for no better reason than that the markets, perceiving the risk of a government U-turn to be much lessened, may not exact the same precautionary premium.

This may, in its turn, encourage us to modify the view of social democratic (and other) governments as increasingly 'powerless' in the face of global market forces. That the range of options open to particular states is constrained and that the extent of those constraints varies from one state to another in line with its geopolitical and economic strength is nothing new. The processes of globalization and even, to some extent, global 'talk' may shift opportunities and costs for policy-makers (among others). But they do not reduce the range of policy options to one, nor can they relieve policy-makers of other pressures, including those that come from organized interests, public opinion, entrenched institutions and the weight of accumulated entitlements and expectations. Even if the pressures of globalization were the same on all states and were to drive them all in the same direction, they would be starting from very different positions and would still be likely to look quite different once the globalization 'shift' had been effected. We now have plenty of evidence that politics and institutions still matter, even, perhaps especially, in the politics of welfare retrenchment (P. Pierson 1994, 1996). To put it simply, if we imagine that the United States and Sweden were to come under just the same pressure to retrench their welfare states and that both responded with substantively similar measures (in themselves, two rather implausible premises), they would both still look quite different at the end of that process.

This may point us towards a further qualification of the globalization story. In some circumstances, it may be that it is politicians or policy-makers who *choose* globalization (rather than the other way around). Of course, this is not a 'free' choice and may be made only because all the alternatives are so unattractive. Nonetheless, it may persuade us to reject the image of state actors rendered 'powerless' by globalization. The first Hawke adminis- tration in Australia introduced an extensive raft of deregulating measures on its election in 1983 (including floating the Australian dollar). This led some to align its practice with the agenda of contemporary Thatcher and Reagan administrations as an early instance of social democratic neoliberalism (C. Pierson, 1998b). But in fact subsequent governments under Hawke and Keating gave considerable attention to the social wage and prosecuted their agenda of micro-economic reform in a series of corporatist accords with the central organs of the Australian trade union movement (ACTU). Again, Fligstein (1998, pp. 30–1) argues that the shift from countercyclical measures to the prioritization of price stability over the past twenty years originated not with the markets but with policy-makers convinced that their previous policies were contributing to uncontrollable domestic price infla- tion. Fear of the reaction of international currency holders was only a part of this story. Indeed, the detailed consideration of any globalization 'episode' reveals complex interplay and feedback as politicians seek to anticipate markets and market actors seek to second-guess the politicians. Both have certain key resources at their disposal but both also face severe external constraints. It is wrong, then, to insist that politicians had no choice, that global- ization pressed upon them an irresistible policy formulation. But, at the same time, globalization was much more than politicians being frightened by their own words and shadows. The room for policy manoeuvre was strictly limited and the room for prefer- ence-shaping policy, of the kind that Hay (1997, 1999) recom- mends, quite small.

Further qualification to the globalizers' argument is provided by Rieger and Leibfried (1998), who argue that as well as globalization placing limits on welfare state development, there are real welfare state limits to globalization. They argue that historically and politically the movement towards a more open trading system has relied on the sorts of structures of compensa- tion that social democratic corporatism (and others) put in place to protect economic 'losers'. Thus the growing openness of the international financial regime after 1945 was premised in part on the social institutions of an 'embedded liberalism'. If the feedback from greater globalization undermines domestic social settlements, it may generate increased opposition to trade openness (presaged in various 'protectionist' strains in contemporary democratic politics). It may be that globalization 'winners' ignore this possibility at their peril, since, as Rodrik notes (1997, p. 7), 'social disintegration is not a spectator sport.'

Furthermore, we should be aware that there is a danger of overestimating the impact of globalization by attributing to it every setback for social democratic forces. Garrett (1998) insists that the reverses experienced by the Swedish economy of the early 1990s were the consequence of the collapse of the Soviet Union plus German reunification plus a botched macro-economic policy, rather than the irresistible press of global forces on an overgenerous social democratic welfare state. Still more instructively, Fligstein (1998, p. 33) argues that the crisis of the Mexican peso in 1994, which appears definitively as a crisis produced by the globalization of international financial markets, was as much the product of domestic and international political decisions and disorders over a period of years. The rapid movement out of the currency may simply have been the final precipitating event in a much longer chain of causation. All the way back to 'the gnomes of Zurich' (and long before), foreign bankers have been blamed for social democratic economic reverses. That there may sometimes have been some truth in these claims does not detract from the fact that, in the politics of blame avoidance, the temptation to attribute misfortune to foreign bankers will always be overwhelmingly attractive.

The impact of a changing division of labour

Finally, we turn to the impact of those recent changes in the international and domestic division of labour that seem to have come in the wake of globalization. We have already seen that most economists accept that the shift in unskilled work from developed to developing worlds has had a real impact on unemployment and/or wage inequality in developed societies, and some have argued that the greater competition *between* the developed economies may also have contributed to greater job insecurity and a weakening of terms and conditions of employment (Cline, 1997; Rodrik, 1997). Certainly, permanent mass unemployment and growing wage disparities are widely regarded as a key challenge for traditional forms of social democratic governance. Still, it remains the case that most economists attribute much the greater part of this decline in unskilled employment (and its consequent effect on wages and employment) to technological change. Deindustrialization may remain just as much of a problem and one which social democratic (and other) governments have had to confront – but not primarily as a consequence of heightened globalization.

In many ways what is more consequential is the extended chain of change in domestic employment (and unionization) which follows from both globalization and the domestic forms of defence taken to address it. The decline of collectivism has been a crucial change for those who have identified globalization with the declining efficacy of social democracy. This decline in collective institutions and values is sometimes seen as part of a much broader (and perhaps irresistible) trend within 'late modernity' towards new forms of individualism (Giddens, 1994). But its most crucial facet for those who perceive globalization as undermining traditional social democracy is the secular decline of trade unionism. In fact, trade unions have always had very variable relationships to 'their' social democratic parties and even the most 'fraternal' of these partnerships have come under duress when social democratic parties have been in government. Nonetheless, unions have been seen at the very least as representing and mobilizing a key interest in the social democratic constituency and often, especially within the more successful social democratic corporatist regimes, as indispensable partners in delivering a coherent redistributive agenda.

Not everyone accepts that a real decline in trade unionism has taken place (at least not within the core social democracies). Garrett (1998), for example, argues that though there has been an overall decline in union densities since their high point (around 1980), this is a far from uniform process and the collapse is much less dramatic than a focus on outliers (such as the US and the UK) would suggest. In three of the 'core' social democratic economies (Sweden, Denmark and Finland) union densities actually rose through the 1980s and 1990s to reach levels in excess of 70 per cent. But in many ways, these social democratic corporatist states are even more atypical (and certainly very much smaller) than Britain and the US (Ebbinghaus and Visser, 2000). There is some evidence that decline in union membership may have 'bottomed out', but in a number of developed OECD states this leaves union densities below 30 per cent (Golden, Wallerstein and Lange, 1999). Recent changes in the composition of the workforce – with growing numbers in small firms, in the service sector and in part-time employment – also generate new (if not insurmountable) problems for trade union organization (C. Pierson, 1995, p. 10).

Quite as significant as the decline in absolute numbers and densities is the pronounced division between unions in the public and private sectors. In most developed economies, union membership is two to three times as high in the public as in the private sector. In a sense all trade unionism is about overcoming the differences of interest that workers have as individuals and enabling them to act collectively. A key difficulty posed by these changes in the disposition of union membership under circumstances of globalization is that workers in the public and private sectors may have interests and forms of representation which increasingly diverge. This is a particular problem for those political economies which rested on a disciplined and centralized trade union movement trading immediate wage increases for long-term investment or increases in the social wage. The problem is that wages for those in the public sector are not subject to the same (external) competitiveness constraint as workers in the traded sector of the economy. The tendency for wage push in the highly organized public sector may impact on the long-term viability of corporatist settlements. At the same time, it may be that workers in the private sector see themselves as better served by negotiating terms and conditions on a sectoral, corporate or even plant-level basis. Certainly Pontusson (1995) claims to have found evidence that the move towards smaller plants and increasing employment in the non-industrial private sector has contributed to a decline in institutional support for social democracy. At the same time, it seems clear that greater capital mobility has reduced the incentives for capital to be involved in domestic corporatist arrangements. It takes two (or three) to intermediate and however dense and organized trade unions may be they are vulnerable to capital simply defecting from corporatist arrangements, as has clearly happened, at least to some degree, in the Swedish case (Pontusson and Swenson, 1996; see also Schwartz, 2000b).

Upon one account, this challenge to collectivist practices and institutions is not a problem but a boon for social democracy. In a carefully constructed argument, Kitschelt (1994, p. 6) rejects the widely held supposition that 'the relative electoral strength and policy-making capacity of social democracy depends on the centralized organization of the working class and its ability to forge alliances with other wage earners.' The close concertation of social democratic parties with strongly centralized trade union organizations, once a virtue, is now 'a liability'. Social democratic parties seeking new voters and innovative policies fare best when they are unshackled from a union movement that is increasingly unable to deliver either votes or labour market clout. To this extent, the weakening of trade unions may, somewhat counter-intuitively, be of advantage to social democrats. But it seems clear that Kitschelt's focus here is principally on the *electoral* prospects for social democracy. By the end of the 1990s we knew, if this was ever in doubt (and clearly for some it was), that social democratic parties *can* still win elections. But there was apparently a substantive price to pay, at least in terms of more traditional social democratic aspirations.

> What remains of social democratic economic leftism is the defense of basic principles of the welfare state, such as the right to a minimum standard of living for all citizens and equal opportunities in the educational system, together with advocacy of a moderate system of income redistribution through taxes and benefits that serve this purpose . . . Social democrats thus lose the capacity to contrast their economies and social policy message to that of the mainstream bourgeois conservative parties. At stake between the parties are only slightly different methods to support and to correct private market allocation of scarce goods. (Kitschelt, 1994, p. 297)

If the goal of social democrats was (just) for social democratic parties to win elections, Kitschelt's argument might run. Those who want to see some further *substantive* agenda in social democracy are likely to find his judgement rather disappointing.

Globalization and social democracy: an assessment

In its most stringent and dramatic form, the logic of globalization seems to render anything more than the most rudimentary system of social welfare or than a completely deregulated labour market quite impossible. If ever hyperglobalization were to be realized, we should all end up with the social protection regime of Chad, the one bright point being that with hypermobility of factors of production the economy of Chad would be growing feverishly as it realized all of its considerable competitive advantages.

These more apocalyptic accounts of globalization are pretty fanciful. Heightened trade has an impact on domestic states but the nature of that impact is ambiguous. At certain times and in some places, greater trade openness has coincided with larger public economies (following the 'compensation' thesis). Capital mobility has increased at an extraordinary pace but it has not been followed by a flood of disinvestment from developed economies (with large public sectors). Indeed, Swank doubted that capital had really seen the sorts of reductions in its overall tax burden that mobility was predicted to bring (largely because capital tends to be attracted by the prospects of profitable investment rather than simply low taxes or low labour costs). A new international division of labour has certainly left its mark on domestic labour markets and corporatist institutions, but there is something of a consensus that technological change has been far more consequential in this area than the transfer of employment into less developed economies.

At the same time, we have plenty of evidence that globalization does make a difference. The abandonment of capital controls does reduce the macro-economic repertoire of domestic governments. Greater mobility does alter the incentives for capital to participate in corporatist arrangements and make 'exit' a less costly option. Tax regimes have become flatter and less progressive. The capacity to operate across borders enhances the powers of multinational corporations. The need to attract and retain foreign investment is an important consideration for national treasuries. Despite his powerful sceptical case, even Garrett (1998, 1999) is forced to concede that globalization has exerted *some* real restraint on policy even within his most favoured social democratic corporatist states in recent years.

On the other hand, globalization need not constitute 'pure loss' for social democratic forces. After all, there are potential welfare gains from trade and these formed the basis of the open economy/extensive welfare state regimes of northern Europe recommended by Garrett. Collapsing costs of communication and transport do more than facilitate instantaneous disinvestment. Nor is it true that the end of the Bretton Woods era has led us into an epoch where international financial and trade arrangements are completely unregulated. Indeed, in many ways, the terrain of 'global governance' is now more crowded and 'enmeshed' than ever. In large part, this is because global markets, like any others, do not make or maintain themselves. Certainly states now share this business of 'global governance' with many other actors. The World Bank, the International Monetary Fund, the World Trade Organization, meetings of the G7 and G8 industrialized economies, large corporations and a range of international non-governmental organizations are all part of this process. Critics usually draw attention to the neoliberal agenda of these organizations and their power to dictate terms to impoverished nations (a function which was once performed by imperialist states). But a subtheme is surely that the global economic order is subject to rules and regulation and, to a limited extent, coordination. The global economy may heighten inequality and foreclose on the options of the disadvantaged, but not because it is unregulated.

We could argue at great length and, in the end, rather inconclusively about whether the bottle marked 'globalization' is half empty or half full. There is a real globalization effect – but it is much less than is widely assumed. In explaining the restraints on social democratic governments, it needs to take its place modestly alongside slowed economic growth, occupational change and the remorseless pressure of demographics (P. Pierson, 1998). There is no unambiguous metric for measuring the impact of globalization. Indeed, if we attend to the question in any detail we see that globalization covers a range of differing processes whose pace and impact will vary quite significantly from state to state. What is crucial, though, is that we recognize that globalization is best understood not in terms of policies which it either 'mandates' or 'prohibits', but rather in terms of changes which it brings about in the structure of costs and opportunities for differing actors. Of course, a truly prohibitive cost constitutes an effective veto, but more generally we should understand the impact of globalization on social democratic states (with which we are especially concerned) as one of redefining the costs and opportunities of particular strategies. It may be that particular policies become more difficult (costly) to pursue or, on the other hand, that the process of coalition formation from within which established policies could be pursued is made more difficult. At the same time, globalization may afford new possibilities, for example by increasing the numbers of those moderately affluent but economically vulnerable people to whom social democratic policies may appeal.

It is important that we understand the problem of social democracy in relation to globalization in this way. First, it reminds us that there are still choices to be made – even if these have become more expensive or more difficult to mobilize. That the range of choices is always limited, that goals may conflict, that pursuit of the best may drive out the good and that, in the end, social democrats may have to choose the lesser of two evils are fairly timeless political commonplaces. As these cost parameters shift, so it may be that old strategies and alliances will give way to new arrangements (for an earlier account of this process, unrelated to globalization, see Esping-Andersen, 1985).

Still more crucially, the failure to see the issue in this way is one of the critical weaknesses of attempts to 'refashion' social democracy or to define a new 'third way'. John Gray's account of this process seems to me simply to be misconceived. Greater trade openness and increased capital mobility can make life difficult for social democracy, but they certainly do not make it impossible. More measured attempts to fashion a 'third way' (most influentially, those of Tony Giddens, 1998, 2000) do not fare very much better. In part, this is because their leading counterfactual – 'traditional social democracy' – is largely a caricature. By taking social democracy to be more or less universally represented by something called 'the Keynesian welfare state', a form which is now taken to be more or less irredeemably 'exhausted', the quest for a third way is made to seem unavoidable. But this argument proceeds too quickly. The idea of a

'Keynesian welfare state' captures only a part of the social democratic experience and its 'exhaustion' is far from straightforward. If Keynesianism simply meant 'government deficit spending to sustain full employment' the case might be made. But if we take Keynesianism to mean 'government intervention in economic life in the recognition that markets are not self-constituting or always maximally efficient', it might still have a lot of work to do. We may enter the same sorts of reservations about the 'exhaustion' of the welfare state. Life has certainly become much more difficult for developed welfare states (and, more especially, their clients) over the past twenty-five years. But they have been surprisingly robust in the face of a sustained challenge. They remain crucial sources of income and well-being for huge numbers of people. When every qualification has been entered, they are still the principal mechanism we have for redistributing wealth (and opportunities).

This is not the same as saying that what social democracy lacks now (as supposedly it always has) is the iron will that can make change happen. I think it is right to say both that globalization matters and that in many ways it has made life much harder for social democrats. What we should challenge is the claim that these changes require that social democracy should simply abandon its traditional quest to marry social justice to economic efficiency.

5

The Challenge of Demographic Change

The other great contemporary challenge to the integrity of social democratic politics is seen to come from processes of demographic change. The social and economic policies of social democracy may have worked in earlier (perhaps simpler and easier) times, but ongoing processes of demographic change are making these ever more difficult to effect. Above all, the social democratic aspiration to use state power (through macro-economic policy and the welfare state) to achieve greater equality and to underpin an expansive conception of social citizenship is unrealizable in the face of these deep-seated social changes. The best social democrats can do is to help citizens to develop marketable assets and create a climate which will encourage investment. Increasingly, it will be up to individuals to look after their own well-being.

As we shall see, contemporary societies are subject to a range of demographic changes – fewer and later marriages, more divorces, smaller families, more single-person households, changing female labour force participation – and the nature and scale of these challenges are subject to considerable international variation. They are also seen to interact in potentially volatile ways with the 'imperatives' of globalization. Although particular attention has come to be focused on one element of change – the consequences of the rapid ageing of societies – we shall see that it is really a cocktail of changes in social and population trends that is so consequential for existing social policy regimes. In this chapter, I consider in some detail the nature and extent of these changes, before turning to an assessment of their consequences for a social democratic politics.

Ageing societies

At its most primitive, the key argument in relation to ageing societies is that at some point in the next fifty years in all developed and many developing countries the costs of supporting a growing elderly population out of the current production of a much smaller active workforce will place on the latter a burden which is either unsustainable or, at the very least, politically unacceptable. At some point in this inexorable process, the implicit 'intergenerational' pact on which welfare state funding depends may collapse – unless governments act now to scale back future public commitments to the elderly. Of course, a concern with the ageing of the population (and its costs) is not entirely new (see, for example, the report of the UK Royal Commission on Population of 1949). Indeed, the need to maintain or enhance fertility rates (as a counterweight to ageing) has frequently been used as an argument for the *expansion* of welfare provision, as, for example, in the call for family allowances and the 'endowment of motherhood' (Folbre, 1994, pp. 157–8; Sauvy, 1969). But in its newest manifestation the key issue is cost containment.

Of decisive importance in promoting this agenda has been the authoritative and proselytizing work of international agencies such as the OECD (1988, 1992, 1998, 1999) and, above all, the World Bank, whose revealingly titled 1994 report *Averting the Old Age Crisis* became required reading in social security ministries (and treasuries) around the globe. Upon the World Bank's account, existing social security programmes are 'beset by escalating costs that require high taxes and deter private sector growth – while failing to protect the old' (1994, p. 1). These programmes have 'spun out of control' and require urgent reform. Almost as interesting, if a little less influential, is the extent to which many of those who are broadly sympathetic to social democratic intentions, and sceptical about the impact on these of globalization, seem persuaded of the intensity of the demographic challenge.

Thus Garrett observes that 'the root causes of the looming welfare state crisis are, in the context of stable working-age populations, significant increases in steady state rates of unemployment and, *more importantly, the growing ranks of the aged population entitled to state pensions and health benefits*' (1998, p. 150; emphasis added). Similarly, Paul Pierson, having surveyed the evidence of societal ageing and the consequent increases in pension and health-care costs, concludes that 'the demographic shift underway is profound . . . the phenomenon of population ageing is slow-moving and undramatic, but it has fundamental consequences over time' (1998, p. 551).

It is tempting to yield on this issue to the weight of established authority. That societies are ageing seems indisputable, as does the only marginally more subjective judgement that, given existing regimes of support for the elderly, this is a process that will prove to be very costly. Since there is a well-grounded suspicion that the only thing duller than thinking about your pension is talking about someone else's, and given the difficulties in making sense of the dizzying array of future options, including the plethora of possible retirement savings instruments, it is tempting to leave the field to those with the appropriate expertise. Nonetheless, this is a quite crucial arena for the future possibilities of social democratic governance. The question is not whether societal ageing represents a challenge. Clearly it does. Rather, as ever, it is a question of degree (how severe is the challenge? how pressing is the call for change?) and, just as crucially, of what options remain open. The issue of affordability was used throughout the twentieth century as a political device to challenge the growth of welfare states. It is used now in the attempt to mandate greater reliance on private provision, less generous benefits and more targeting (all developments seemingly counterposed to the 'classical' social democratic welfare state). We cannot properly avoid making at least some provisional judgements about the real nature and extent of the ageing crisis, about which, as we shall see, even the actuarially well informed are not in uniform agreement.

Much of the challenge of ageing will be most acutely felt in those less developed states where change is most rapid and resources most limited. By 2030, for example, one-quarter of the world's old people will be living in China (World Bank, 1994,

p. 33). But in reviewing what we may call the new orthodoxy of population ageing, I shall focus on those more advanced economies in which welfare states and social democracy have been most developed.

Old age crisis: the World Bank and the new orthodoxy

It makes sense to begin any survey of current thinking on the dynamics of ageing and its consequences for both economic and social policy with a consideration of the World Bank's 1994 report *Averting the Old Age Crisis*. This is not just an authoritative and influential statement of the new orthodoxy but has also played its part in ratcheting up expectations of an impending crisis. The World Bank report sets the scene with some alarming statistics. In 1990, almost half a billion people in the world's population (about 9 per cent) were aged 60 or over. By 2030, this number is projected to nearly triple to 1.4 billion (16 per cent). Developing societies are ageing much more rapidly than their industrialized precursors. Doubling of the elderly population which took 140 years in France will occur in just 34 years in China and 22 years in Venezuela (World Bank, 1994, p. 1). At the same time, increasing life expectancies mean that there will be a growing number of 'older elderly' people (conventionally defined as those over 75 or 80) on whom many of the health and nursing care costs of ageing are concentrated. In the OECD area, for example, the population over 75 is set to double between 1990 and 2030 and this older section of the aged population is likely to continue to be made up disproportionately of women, whose economic status tends to be worse than that of older men (OECD, 1996, p. 103; World Bank, 1994, pp. 28–30).

The other key demographic development in the coming half-century is the worsening elderly dependency ratio, that is the ratio between this growing aged population and the numbers of those of working age (defined as those between 15 and 64) out of whose productive activity the consumption needs of the elderly will be met. In the OECD as a whole, the elderly dependency ratio is set to rise from 19 per cent to 37 per cent between 1990 and 2030 – a near doubling in just forty years.[1] For some states, the transformation is still more dramatic, with

Japan's dependency ratio tripling by 2030, and the ratio increasing to more than 40 per cent in both Germany and Italy (OECD, 1996, p. 103). Although projections across a range of states vary quite significantly, simply to maintain existing patterns of entitlement would require pension expenditures in the most severely affected OECD states (Japan, Italy and Germany) to rise to above 15 per cent of GDP at some time in the next fifty years (OECD, 1996, p. 33).

Pension reform

According to the World Bank's account, however, the problem is not just one of unfavourable demographic change. Indeed, rather more is it that most existing pension regimes will end up making the situation worse, not better. This is because most systems of old age security are based on mandatory public schemes financed by payroll taxes and provided on a pay-as-you-go (PAYG) basis (James, 2000, pp. 271–2). Under such a regime, today's workers pay today's pensions in what has, up until now, been the confident expectation that when the time comes, their pensions will be paid by the next generation of workers. This system may work reasonably well, so it is argued, while the pensioner population is relatively small and growth in earnings makes worker contributions affordable and enables retired people to share in the general benefits of economic growth. However, when the demographic profile becomes less favourable, or wage growth falters, it sets in train a vicious circle. The increasing demand for resources to fund the pensions of a growing retired population must be met either out of the incomes of existing workers or their employers or by a growth in public debt.

None of these solutions is satisfactory. Increasing the burden on the present generation of workers is unfair and may, indeed, prove regressive if costs borne by the comparatively low-paid in the present generation are used to pay the pensions of even quite affluent older people. Such impositions are likely to be resisted either politically or by decreased economic participation in the formal economy (the level of payroll taxes acting as a disincentive to enter the labour market). Workers who exclude themselves from the formal economy will, of course, fail to build up their own entitlement to social insurance benefits and increase the pressure on those who do contribute. If it were possible to transfer these payroll costs entirely to employers (though most economists seem to believe that, in the end, it is workers who fund these payments) this would result in lower employment (especially in an environment where capital could be invested elsewhere), less investment and lowered economic growth. Personal savings would be depressed and other and more productive forms of public expenditure (for example, investment in infrastructure or education) would be crowded out. Countries that sought to fund their growing pension commitment through increasing public indebtedness would find their behaviour punished by international financial markets and end up with an increasing amount of GDP devoted to the entirely unproductive business of servicing the public debt. In the end, only economic growth can 'square the circle' of raising living standards for both retired and economically active populations, but the dynamics of PAYG regimes are such as to distort economic incentives and further restrict economic growth.

Transition

The World Bank's 'solution' combines a reduction in the public commitment to pensions provision with reforms designed to raise levels of economic activity and, with it, the overall pool of resources out of which the needs of future generations of workers and retirees must be met. The Bank's recommendation involves moving to a three-pillared system of old-age social security. The public pillar should provide a flat or means-tested pension or a minimum pension guarantee. Its principal aim should be to provide a 'social safety net' and prevent poverty. It would be mandatory, tax funded and index-linked to either wages or prices (or some combination thereof). Especially if it was combined with a raising of the retirement age, the reformed public pillar should prove much less costly than existing PAYG systems. The second pillar would also be mandatory but it would be fully funded and privately managed. Workers would contribute either to occupational plans provided by their employers or else to their own private pension schemes. The Bank's preference is for a defined contribution (DC) scheme in which the sum out of which a pension was funded at maturity would reflect the cumulative value of sums invested in the fund, rather than, as in a defined benefit (DB) scheme, a formula based on final salary. The expectation is that access to equity markets would allow workers to participate more fully in the benefits of economic growth. Indeed their increased savings would provide the capital that would help to fuel such economic growth. In contrast to public schemes, 'competitively managed, funded pension plans . . . are more likely to enjoy the benefits of investment diversification, that protects them against inflation and other risks, and to spur financial market development, thereby enhancing economic growth' (James, 2000, p. 277). There would be a further fully funded voluntary pillar (which might or might not receive favourable tax treatment) for those who wished to increase their investment for retirement beyond that mandated in the second compulsory-but-private pillar.

Perhaps the trickiest issue of all in the World Bank's proposed reform is the transition from what we have to what they recommend. In essence, the challenge is to move from a PAYG system (in which the current working generation pay for the pensions of those now retired) to a system where workers largely pre-fund their own retirement incomes (through contributions into a fully funded mandatory second pension) without imposing on one generation the double burden of paying for both their own pensions and that of the preceding generation. The Bank presents a number of ingenious (or perhaps disingenuous) devices for moderating this problem. But even on their most optimistic projections (with reform generating much higher economic growth rates, drastically reducing previous levels of evasion, etc.), it is, in the end, an issue of sharing out the disappointment – delaying retirement, paying lower replacement rates, while increasing taxes and social security charges. The Bank concedes that there is no way to secure the necessary reforms within a viable time-scale without disappointing the reasonable expectations of some part of the population and, indeed, without governments reneging on commitments they have already made to their citizens. Despite this, they hope that it may prove possible to mobilize a consensus for reform through a publicity campaign demonstrating that 'there is no alternative' (World Bank, 1994, pp. 255–92).

The OECD and 'the new social policy agenda'

Ageing societies

The turn of the millennium policy statement of the Organization for Economic Co-operation and Development (OECD, 1999) covers some of the same ground as the World Bank's 1994 report but its demographic concerns are cast a little wider and its style – in keeping with its title, *A Caring World* – is a little gentler. In line with the OECD's own promotion of a more 'active' society (and a more 'active' welfare state to match), the key ambition of the 'new' social policy is 'to achieve social solidarity through enabling individuals and families to support themselves' and this is to be achieved, above all, by promoting 'employment-oriented welfare policies' (1999, p. 4).

On the issue of ageing, the OECD draws attention to the evidence of growing longevity, rising dependency ratios and an escalating implicit public pension debt. It endorses the view that the status quo is not an option and supports calls for reductions in public pension benefits, increases in contributions and a move towards more advance-funded pension schemes. In line with its employment-oriented remit, it also pays particular attention to the secular decline in economic participation rates among older workers (particularly men in the age group 55–64). Participation rates for the 55–64 year old group and effective retirement ages fell significantly between 1950 and 1980, while life expectancies rose, and in a number of countries early retirement or a transfer of older workers from unemployment benefits to disability allowances was more or less consciously employed as an instrument of government policy (OECD, 1996, pp. 65–80). The OECD presses for a reversal of this trend, encouraging the fuller participation of older workers by removing existing financial incentives for early retirement. This fuller participation of older workers is seen as a way of significantly reducing the burden of pension (and associated social security) costs.

The OECD recommends three further measures to address the pensions challenge: (1) incrementally *raising the age of retirement* and encouraging those who wish to work beyond this age to do so, perhaps on a part-time basis; (2) promoting *general cost containment* by reducing replacement rates, moderating the effects of benefits indexing, requiring longer contribution periods for full benefits, etc.; and (3) *targeting benefits* either explicitly through a means test or by increasing the liability of benefits to taxation. At the same time, contributions could be increased by raising levels or increasing the proportion of earnings which are liable for payroll taxation, though the OECD is clearly conscious of the threat that higher non-wage labour costs (or the 'labour tax wedge') present to a social policy based on maximum involvement in paid employment (OECD, 1996, 1999).

Health and long-term care

It is routinely assumed that an ageing population will place increasing pressure on health-care systems and regimes of long-term residential and community care. This is based on the greater incidence of morbidity in the elderly, particularly among the very old. (Across a range of OECD countries, heath-care expenditures are on average two and half times as high for those over sixty-five as for the younger population). Much higher ratios (up to five times the spend on the more youthful populations) are reported for those over seventy-five. The health cost consequences of ageing may not quite be linear. There is evidence that the health status of the 'young elderly' may not be so very much different from that of the general population and some evidence that the most costly health-care interventions are heavily concentrated on the last one or two years of life *whenever these may come* (OECD, 1996, pp. 51–64). Optimists are also inclined to argue that coming generations of elderly will reach old age in better health than their predecessors, be better informed about the maintenance of their health and be generally more attuned to healthier lifestyles. Counteracting this is the extent to which medical advances have converted what would once have been fatal disorders into chronic long-term conditions which can be very costly to treat. Overall, the OECD projects that ageing will lead to some increase in public health-care costs over the next forty years. These increases are significant but still comparatively modest, adding perhaps around 2 per cent of GDP across the period (1996, pp. 56–9).

More intractable is the problem of long-term care for the frail elderly. Here existing provision is more piecemeal and funding regimes are less clearly established. Traditional patterns of family support for the frail and vulnerable elderly are seen to be in decline and there is evidence of growing numbers of elderly people living alone, though this is a trend which may be flattening out (OECD, 1999, pp. 18–20). The OECD's view seems to be that, whether funded through the public or the private sector, the prospect of long-term care in old age needs to be recognized as a normal risk for the entire population and therefore as a contingency for which all should be (socially or privately) insured.

The changing role of women

While it is the social policy consequences of ageing (on pensions, health provision and long-term care) that have attracted the greatest attention, demographic changes have also pressed on other areas of social provision. Many of these changes relate to the transformed social and economic role of women. Despite substantial international variations, we can say generally that, since the 1960s, women have become increasingly active in formal labour markets. In 1964, the participation rate ranged from around 25 per cent in Ireland and Spain to around 50 per cent in Britain. In 1994, participation rates were between 70 and 80 per cent in the Scandinavian countries, and only in Ireland and Spain were they still below 50 per cent. Although in some states (Britain is a notable example) women were disproportionately to be found in part-time work, there was also a secular increase in women's full-time employment. There was also a clear move away from that pattern in which women would withdraw from the workforce for extended periods while they had children of school age. At the same time, there was a move for women to marry later, to be older at the time of the birth of the first child and to have lower completed fertility rates (OECD, 1997, pp. 46–7). Indeed, completed fertility rates are now well below replacement levels (roughly 2.1) in a number of OECD countries, including Italy (1.63) and Spain (1.69). If not reversed, this decline in fertility rates will generate substantial declines in population (and an intensification of societal ageing). Evidence suggests that women are waiting until they have completed their (extended) education and perhaps establishing careers before having children and that completed family sizes are becoming smaller (see Castles, 1998, pp. 264–78). This growing involvement of women in paid labour has also helped to contribute to a characteristic division in contemporary labour markets between work-rich and work-poor households, that is between those family households in which both parents are working and those in which no member of the household has paid employment (OECD, 1999, p. 23).

Lone parents

The only demographic change to have rivalled ageing as a source of moral panic in recent years has been the growth in the numbers of single-parent families. In the US, for example, the dependency of single mothers on welfare (and the delinquency of absentee fathers) has generated an enormous degree of interest and controversy (see, for example, Mead, 2000; Murray, 2000). Although the response has sometimes seemed disproportionate, there has been a substantial growth in the numbers of lone-parent households. By the 1990s, a quarter of all households with dependent children in the US and in New Zealand had a single head. In the UK, Canada, Austria and Norway, the figure was around a fifth. The number of children born to unmarried mothers has also risen sharply, though unevenly (to over a third in the UK). Over 90 per cent of non-widow, lone-parent families are headed by mothers and there is a disproportionate likelihood that these families (and the children within them) will be living in poverty (Saraceno, 1997, pp. 84–5).

Although the treatment of single parents (and the generosity shown towards them) has varied a great deal, there has always been a tension between seeing sole parents as breadwinners and/ or as carers. Many welfare regimes have sanctioned single mothers' non-participation in the formal labour market while they had responsibility for their children, but not generally in ways which have given households headed by a lone parent economic parity with other household types. Those who have wished to enter the workforce have often been discouraged by a mixture of low pay and expensive childcare. Increasingly, the OECD's emphasis, given its general remit of an 'employment-oriented social policy' in the context of an 'active society', has been on encouraging single parents into the formal labour market. Potentially, policy-makers have available a mixture of carrots (better and cheaper childcare, in-work benefits for the low paid, education and training opportunities) and sticks (more intrusive case management, lower and more restricted benefits). Recent evidence (from reform proposals in the UK and Australia) suggests attempts to broaden the range of opportunities, but in a context of more compulsion (DfEE, 2000; Dean, 1998).

The disabled

A broadly similar policy mix can be found in the case of the disabled of working age. As we have observed, a number of states used 'incapacity for work' and its attendant benefits system as a mechanism for removing older workers from the world of work (or, more usually, the rolls of the unemployed). Recent years have seen a 'tightening up' of disability regimes in a number of countries (notably in the UK and the Netherlands), with significant reductions in the populations regarded as relevant (see Visser, 1998). At the same time, governments have committed themselves to making greater efforts to ensure that the disabled are integrated into the active workforce (often under the rubric of 'social inclusion'), at times drawing on the claims for recognition among organizations of the disabled themselves.

The new life course

Overall, the OECD recommends a range of policies to address the 'new life course'. Compared with the position some forty years ago, men and women both live considerably longer. For men, fewer years are spent working; for women, the reverse is true. Both men and women are likely to spend longer in formal education and in retirement. For the OECD, the consequences of these changes are twofold: 'policy interventions should be targeted at the points where they have most impact, so reducing social and labour market dysfunctioning; and a better balance needs to be struck between time spent in learning, working, caring and leisure.' Among the most important innovations this suggests are an emphasis on 'lifetime learning' and 'active ageing', heavier investment in early-years learning, greater attention to the transition from education to work and increasing flexibility in the policy approach to differing mixes of care, education, work and leisure spread across individual life-cycles. An element of redistribution may be defended – but this is principally as a necessary by-product of relieving poverty or destitution rather than as a desirable end in itself and should interfere as little as possible with the dynamics that make economies grow. The incidence of poverty is still recognized as an occasion for action but this is frequently recast under the rather more dynamic rubric of social exclusion. Whether for the individual or the household, *long-term* poverty remains a problem but the prevailing argument is that it may be better to have a large number of low-paid entry-level jobs (in the hope of putting their holders on to the jobs escalator) than a wages floor that restricts employment.

Evaluating the 'new social policy agenda'

Our substantive interest in this chapter is in assessing the space that is left or, indeed, opened up for a social democratic politics by recent demographic changes. Before we can enter such a judgement, we need to consider the plausibility and authority of the cases set out by the World Bank and the OECD. Both organizations seek to represent their arguments as largely technocratic rather than political and their conclusions as more or less unavoidable (at least for any policy-maker who does not want to court disaster). Given the nature and scale of the demographic changes outlined, so it is argued, partisanship is largely irrelevant in determining the sorts of institutional choices and incentive structures that governments need to put in place. Cost containment, greater targeting and the displacement of welfare effort from the public to the private sector are all key elements of this newer agenda. History teaches us to be sceptical of arguments that proceed from 'neutral and technocratic' principles to policy conclusions that are both 'inevitable' and apparently mandate a very significant reallocation of costs and resources. A preliminary step, then, is to consider whether we do indeed have to accept that the 'new social policy agenda' sets the legitimate parameters within which social democratic (or any other) politics may be pursued.

In fact, there are plenty of dissenting voices from *within* the relevant policy community.[2] In terms of the World Bank's proposals, a number of commentators point to the considerable downside involved in opting for fully funded defined contribution pensions. The argument here is that risks which were quite properly pooled through the state and the apparatus of social insurance would be displaced on to individual worker-savers. The responsibility for making very complex and hugely consequential decisions are thus devolved to individuals who, with even the most expert (and perhaps costly) advice, will find it extraordinarily difficult to make rational choices. It is an area where an asymmetry of information and knowledge seems unavoidable. At the same time, pensioners with identical contributions records may find themselves with widely differing pension entitlements and standards of living (depending on the performance of those funds with which they have invested). This element of 'luck' may be acceptable for peoples' discretionary income. It is not clear that it will be seen as acceptable in securing their basic retirement income. Annuitization of savings also presents problems, especially if pensioners are obliged to purchase annuities at the point of retirement (when again values will be determined by immediate market conditions). Given their longer life expectancies, women ought to receive a lower annuity than men investing the same sum. Some states have legislated to equalize this anomaly (as in the US), and it is not clear why this equalizing principle should not be applied to iron out other 'anomalies' in the retirement system. There is also a possibility that within a system of mandatory private savings 'too much' capital will be saved or that the regulatory structure surrounding pension investments will mean that funds are managed too conservatively (thus failing to realize in full the anticipated bonus in terms of accelerated economic growth). Nor is it clear, despite the protestations of the World Bank report, that pensioners will be better protected against renewed inflation under a fully privatized scheme.

It appears that the merits of PAYG and fully funded systems are, at least in part, related to the respective growth in returns to either capital or labour (Aaron, 1966). Recent years have seen a shift in favour of investment income, favouring a fully funded regime, but a declining working age population plus a wealth of mandated investment funds might change this relationship in the future. Nor is the management of private pensions regimes without its problems. The UK has a mature financial system and a longstanding tradition of occupational pensions in the private sector. Yet British experience of the drive to extend private pension coverage was marked by wholesale mis-selling and high charges, and proved peculiarly inappropriate for those on lower (but not the very lowest) wages (Waine, 1995). In practice, states will have to provide extensive income support to those with a history of no wages or low wages, and they will require an extensive and sophisticated regulatory apparatus (which will need to be funded) and a regulatory structure (determining the kinds of investments pension funds may make) which will reduce the likely profitability of the funds themselves. Mandating private individuals to commit a certain proportion of their income to saving instruments within a particular (and perhaps conservative) regulatory regime may actually dampen potential capital accumulation. There are potentially problems of legitimacy and authority, too, for states that require citizens to hand over a (significant) part of their income to a private investor but provide no guarantee of the returns that the citizen may expect from such a fund.

All of this is before we consider the difficult question of transition and the double burden (of paying present and future pensions) which must, in however mediated a form, be placed on one or more transitional generations. (There is a natural and reasonable disposition to seek to spread the pain of systemic change, but the more the costs are dispersed, the less effective the reform will be.) As Paul Pierson points out (1998), pension reform generally makes for poor politics. Proposed reforms mean a large-scale reallocation of future resources and entitlements. In a democratic polity, the promise to increase costs and reduce benefits for a broad swathe of the population is likely to be resisted, as popular mobilizations in France and Italy in the mid-1990s seem to suggest (Pitruzzello, 1997). Social democrats are likely to be unnerved by a reform which sets up different communities of interest for those whose pension entitlement is almost entirely in the private sector (but who are the largest contributors to personal taxation) and a much less affluent group which will still be (in their case, wholly) reliant on the state for an income in old age.

There is also a reasonable suspicion that the prospects of an unreformed future are made to look as frightening as possible at least in part to add imagined value to the trade-off between a little unpleasantness now and the prospect of catastrophic breakdown in the future. Thus, while future projections of the aged population may be quite accurate and future dependency ratios only a little less so, the economic consequences of these changes are rather less certain. For example, future projections are sensitive to the compounding of quite small variations in rates of economic growth and to changes in levels of labour force participation. (Thus, for example, the consequences of an aged dependency ratio of 3:1 will be quite different where the labour force participation of the 15–64 age group is at 80 per cent rather than 60 per cent.) Again, quite incremental changes in effective retirement ages make a potentially substantial difference to effective dependency rates, and ageing may in any case change patterns of economic behaviour in ways that counteract the increasing number of elderly persons. Fougere and Merette, for example, insist that 'population ageing could create more opportunities for future generations to invest in human capital formation, which would stimulate economic growth and reduce significantly the apprehended impact of ageing on output per capita' (1999, p. 411). The scale of these changes could be very substantial (see, for example, the projected changes in Italy; Fougere and Merette, 1999, p. 425). The modelling of projected demographic change also indicates that adjustments to savings rates (generally, it is assumed that pensioners dis-save) may not be so perverse as is often assumed and that anticipated increases in taxation may also be much more modest than projections of the 'aged burden' have suggested.

Other changes may not be just as the World Bank and OECD have assumed. Some have argued that the impact of improving health among the elderly may do more to offset the impact of ageing (though we have already seen that the growth in health expenditures arising from ageing are projected to be quite modest). Societal ageing, for example, is not just a reflection of the growing number of older people. It is as much, perhaps in industrialized countries rather more, an aspect of fertility (that is, population replacement rates). We know that in general fertility rates have fallen quite steeply in developed societies in recent decades and that this is part of the problem of ageing (especially in countries such as Italy, Spain and Germany). But we also know (Castles, 1998, pp. 264–78) that the relationship between fertility and female labour force participation has been changing and that those societies with a more generous system of family support have generally seen a lesser decline in fertility. Of course, there is no straightforward relationship between expenditure on childcare provision and fertility. (The history of states 'endowing' motherhood in the hope that it would persuade women to produce more babies is long but largely unsuccessful.) There is, however, enough of a relationship to believe that policy *may* have an effect on the decision to have children and, through this, on the overall demographic profile of the population. Also contentious but consequential is the impact of migration. Politicians, particularly those who have earned a little electoral credit by being 'tough' on immigration, may not regard this as an attractive option. In the years of welfare austerity it has been much more common for politicians to argue that immigration is a luxury that cannot be afforded (see Golding and Middleton, 1982). But most if not all economists tend to follow the line taken by Razin and Sadka (1999) that, with a dynamic model of the economy, immigration is likely to represent a net benefit to all citizens – certainly in terms of the affordability of pensions.

Other challenges are less easy to quantify. Health-care costs seem certain to rise, both in real terms and as a proportion of GDP. This will continue a trend that dates back to the 1960s (OECD, 1999, p. 47). But many states (with rather different health-care regimes) have already introduced cost-cutting reforms – including increased co-payments (where costs are shared between patients and the state) and incentives for greater private provision – and public health-care expenditures have actually been fairly stable since the mid-1980s. Ironically, it is those states with the most extensive public provision that have often been most successful in controlling costs, as the frequently made contrast between the US and the UK suggests (Moran, 1999).

Predicting the future incidence of lone-parent households – and hence the scale of the policy challenge they represent – is tricky. A whole generation of US welfare legislation has been premised on the belief that, in this area, changing incentives will alter behaviour (O'Connor, Orloff and Shaver, 1999, pp. 117–20).

The supposition is that young unmarried women can be dissuaded from having children by altering the structure of the welfare system. While this case remains to be proved, we do know that both the incidence and the rate of growth of single-parent households vary quite substantially between developed states. They are generally much higher in English-speaking countries, while in a number of Scandinavian countries the number of single-parent families actually *fell* during the 1980s (OECD, 1999, p. 18). The appropriate conclusion is probably not to try to predict what the incidence of lone motherhood will be in 2030, but rather to counsel *against* making any such projection too definitive. (Consider how William Beveridge might have fared in making a similar forward projection in the late 1940s.)

Finally, we need to remind ourselves that, whether public or private, the consumption needs of future generations of pensioners (and other net beneficiaries) will have to be met from current economic output. Fully funded pensions *may* have the twin virtues of encouraging faster economic growth (so that the pie out of which the pensioners' slice must come will be larger) and/ or of persuading current savers to commit more resources because of a confidence that their future entitlement is more secure (since the promise comes from a stockbroker and not a politician!). As with Australia's compulsory superannuation, mandatory contributions to private pension funds may avoid the stigma attached to personal taxation and may help to buffer politicians (at least a little) from popular demands for increasing pension income (see C. Pierson, 1998b). But, in the end, affordability will strongly reflect economic performance and, in practice, all pension regimes will involve a mix of private and public provision. There may well be a feedback between social policy and economic performance but levels of growth will also be affected by contingencies entirely outside the scope of social policy.

With all these qualifications in place, the 'unanswerable' case for immediate and radical reform looks a little less compelling. This is just as well, since experience suggests that, however strong the political will to reform may be, change in the social policy area is resolutely incremental and path dependency is strong (P. Pierson, 1998). As ever, it is the largest, most costly programmes (with the most beneficiaries) that are hardest to cut. The one 'virtue' of gradual pension reform as a political practice is that many of its costs may be concealed and postponed into a future which electors may discount even more strongly than politicians. Nonetheless, many states have moved to retrench their provision: raising the retirement age (UK, New Zealand, Italy, Japan), increasing the qualifying period for a full pension (France, Portugal, Ireland, Finland), lowering the basis for upgrading benefits (UK, France, Spain) and income testing the pension (Austria, Denmark, Australia). Parallel changes have been introduced in respect of disability benefits, unemployment protection and family allowances (see C. Pierson, 1998a, p. 164). But overall the impact of the reform agenda has been rather variable.

At first sight rather strangely, it is one of the states best placed to face the challenge of ageing, the UK (with its modestly ageing profile and its established system of funded pensions), that has embraced the reform agenda with particular enthusiasm. Thus New Labour's 1999 Green Paper *Partnership in Pensions* projected a *fall* by 1 per cent in the proportion of GDP devoted to public spending on pensions by 2050 (from 5.5 to 4.5 per cent), with 60 per cent of pensioner income expected to come from private pensions (DSS, 1999, p. 8). In fact what we see, rather less surprisingly, is that it is those states in which change is easiest to effect (because of existing private provision, a more favourable ageing profile and a governing system that facilitates change) rather than those where it is most urgent that have been the most active reformers. At the same time, we need to remember that there are plenty of reasons other than demography for states to be pursuing these reforms. In much of the European Union, for example, the desire to meet the public debt reduction criteria for membership of the single European currency was a more proximate cause of (attempted) pension reform in the mid and late 1990s (Pitruzzello, 1997). Again, while the demographic imperative is one source of motivation for labour market reforms and 'lifelong learning', this is probably subordinate to a persistent concern with long-term joblessness and the call for greater 'competitiveness'.

The policy and politics of demographic change: an assessment

In turning to an assessment of the impact that demographic change has on social democratic politics, we need to distinguish two issues. First, we need to establish, in so far as we can, the nature and extent of the general challenge which demographic change represents for all developed societies and, by a fairly simple extension, for any and all of its governing institutions. Only then can we proceed to consider the particular nature of the challenge that confronts social democratic political forces. There certainly are governing challenges that arise from demographic change. What we want to know is whether there are some challenges that *only* social democratic forces will have to confront (for whatever reason) or whether the challenges which all governing forces will have to confront are likely to present especially acute difficulties for social democrats. If there are no 'special' social democratic problems with demographic change, just those that any governing force would have to confront, this will hardly count as a knock-down argument against confronting the problems using social democratic tools (though obviously it does mean that there is still a real issue about how the job is to be done).

By now it should be clear that there is not one demographic challenge but several, that the certainty with which we can project outcomes varies significantly between these differing spheres and that the scale of the challenges also varies quite substantially between countries (even when we confine our attention to the most developed states). To proceed then, we have to disaggregate a little.

Clearly, the most robust predictions are those that relate to the growth in the elderly population (since this is largely counting persons who are already born), though even here it is necessary to distinguish between *individual ageing* (people living longer) and *population ageing* (the greater proportion of elderly persons within a given population). Individual life expectancy in the OECD is projected to rise by around five years between 1990 and 2030, but it is the way in which this trend interacts with fertility and net migration that really defines the demographic challenge of ageing. In particular, it is the combination of 'baby boom' followed by 'baby bust', alongside the assumption that large-scale immigration is politically infeasible, that generates the particular problem in the first half of the twenty-first century (and its significant moderation thereafter) (OECD, 1996, p. 104). The real scale of the challenge is less easy to measure. In part it depends on the feedback effects of interventions already taken (including commitments to raise the retirement age).

Affordability is also, of course, closely related to medium-term economic performance. As Paul Pierson (1998) points out, the funding difficulties of welfare states in the last twenty years have much more to do with declining rates of economic growth than with profligate governments. At the same time, long-term projections of the costs of welfare states are extremely sensitive to quite modest variations in projected rates of growth. As John Hills (1997) pointed out in the context of the UK, the costs of uprating pensioners' benefits in line with the increase in earnings over the next fifty years (a commitment rejected by both major parties as prohibitively expensive) would add roughly 4 per cent to GDP, the same as the increase experienced in the welfare budget in three years of recession in the early 1990s. Of course, a part of the case for reform is that changes in the funding of pensions can increase savings levels, investment and hence economic growth, ensuring an expansion of the resource base out of which the costs of future provision for elderly populations will have to be met. But the extent of this knock-on increment in economic growth is keenly disputed (see various contributions to OECD, 1992).

The scale of this challenge varies between states. For individual countries, it is a complex mixture of the rapidity of demographic change, absolute levels of affluence, prospects for economic growth and the capacity of governing institutions to deliver reform. The politics of pension reform is difficult and its feasibility is likely to vary according to institutional context. As we saw in the British case, it is possible that reforms may be easiest to pursue where they are least needed. Our survey also showed that ageing was associated with other (costly) changes. Health-care costs are disproportionately focused on the elderly (and especially the older elderly). The growing numbers of frail elderly people without informal carers also present an extensive (and potentially an expensive) challenge in terms of the provision of institutional and non-institutional care (see Scherer, 1996).

Undoubtedly, the 'greying' of societies is a real public policy challenge and the attention devoted to it is well merited. But the precise nature of the challenge between now and 2030 is a little harder to specify. Those who have been pressing the agenda for reform have good reason not to understate the nature of the problem and, in the hands of the rather less cautious, this has sometimes contributed to the rather apocalyptic vision of a 'demographic timebomb' or 'generation wars'. More sober commentators, including those international agencies we have focused on, avoid this type of language (Scherer, 1996). In societies which will be even more affluent by 2030 the answer to the question 'can we afford to grow old?' is unequivocally 'yes'.

Of course, ageing is not the only important element in the 'demographic' challenge. Critical attention has also been directed towards the economic status – and increasingly the *employment* status – of people who are not old, especially lone parents, the long-term unemployed and young people in the transition from education to work. These concerns are connected to a wider framework of social change – rising levels of divorce, 'second families', the increase in 'non-standard' and single-person households, heightened job insecurity, the changing proportion of grandparents to grandchildren. Above all, and impacting on many of these other developments, is the changing social and economic role of women. Most notably, female participation in the formal labour market has been transformed over the past twenty-five years (O'Connor, Orloff and Shaver, 1999). The policy agenda set by these many (and often interacting) social and economic changes is neatly captured by Giddens when he speaks of 'a politics of second chances' (Giddens, 1994, p. 172). Social policy regimes built around the standardized life-cycle and gender settlement of a passing age are likely to fail in a context of rapid (and somewhat open-ended) demographic change. Yet it is as much this *uncertainty* as the expectation of particular changes that we have to seek to write into future social and economic policy.

The demographic challenge and social democracy

In so far as we can make any simple generalization on the basis of this wide diversity of experiences and projections, we can say that demographic change presents developed states with a range of deep-seated challenges and some unenviable choices. For most states, this suggests a process of reform which is incremental and measured. (A more severe challenge might arise from the interaction of the consequences of ageing with ecological limits to growth, but this is an issue that has hardly been registered at the institutional level, though it is raised by Giddens). The issue we must now address is whether demographic change presents a distinctive and more acute problem for social democratic politics. Is there a special 'premium' or 'penalty' for addressing the issue of demographic change within the framework of a social democratic politics?

Of course, this very much depends on where the parameters of a social democratic politics are drawn. As we have seen, Giddens's third way is presented as a 'renewal' of social democracy. As such, it sits quite comfortably within the new paradigm of an 'active society' and 'employment-oriented social policies'. But we saw also that Giddens's makeover relies on a rejection of much of what passed for 'old style' social democracy, including the reconfiguration of *equality* to refer to *inclusion*, now seen as a principle that concerns not the distribution of wealth but rather attachment to 'the social mainstream' (Giddens, 1998, p. 104). Giddens makes similarly accommodating moves to downplay the role of the state, redistribution (at least of resources rather than opportunities) and public provision. Is such a reformulation the only way in which social democracy can be saved from and for itself?

At the very least, we should say that this is an open question. Whoever governs, the challenges which we have considered under the rubric of globalization and demographic change are profound. At the same time, their severity varies very considerably between states. Given the generally incremental nature of the policy changes that are likely to be introduced (particularly in the most costly area of pensions), and the differences in existing regime types, both the differential urgency of the reform agenda and the institutional structure of reforms that emerge are likely to leave a pattern of considerable international variation. Even if policy convergence proves to be a real and sustained process, it will still leave a range of differing policy regimes as its outcome. Must these regimes at least be 'less' social democratic than those we have at present? Circumstances of 'permanent austerity' (if these are what we face) will certainly make it harder to be a 'good' social democrat. Rapid economic growth and fullish employment – like a favourable ageing profile – tend to make political choices easier for everyone. But we should be reluctant to accept the claim that social democratic politics is just a politics of 'good times'. Allocating (comparative) disadvantage fairly is at least as important as the equitable distribution of a growing social product, probably more so. (And behind this lies the recognition that we are thinking about the allocation of goods and opportunities in societies which by historical and, for many, contemporary standards are fabulously wealthy.) Of course, social democrats will be obliged (as they always have been) to attend to the economic context within which they operate. Given that, there is no *prima facie* reason to suppose that the only way in which a social democratic politics can survive in the twenty-first century is by redefining its ambitions to coincide with those of the leading institutions of global economic governance.

6

The Social Democratic Future

In the introduction, I raised three possible responses to the current state of the social democratic enterprise: to give up, to seek out a 'third way' or to 'adapt to survive'. Having considered in some detail the sorts of evidence that ought to inform such a judgement, in this closing chapter I return to an assessment of these three options. I begin by considering seven widely voiced reasons for abandoning the social democratic endeavour altogether.

(1) Social democracy lacks its own distinctive and viable political economy For some critics, the decisive vitiating weakness of social democracy is that, given the profound changes in economy and society of the last thirty years, it no longer has a viable and distinctive strategy for managing economic life. The solutions which social democrats might once have reached are now deemed, for the most part, to be economically illiterate and politically undoable. Increasing demand through a little judicious cutting of taxes and a little more deficit spending is rendered counterproductive by the response of international markets. Letting social expenditure do much of the work of redistribution is incompatible with the need for a 'non-distorting' tax regime. The capacity of the public sector to create employment is exhausted. Since Keynesianism is held no longer to work (for its critics the crucial lesson of the 'stagflation' of the 1970s), social democracy

is left without a political economy of its own. Globalization and the accelerating pace of demographic change simply reveal still more transparently this black hole at the centre of social democratic ambitions. The newer agenda of the World Bank and the OECD is about containing public expenditure and improving the efficiency, flexibility and transparency of markets for both capital and labour. This is seen to run in precisely the opposite direction to the traditional political economy of 'classical' social democracy. Under these circumstances, Social Democratic parties have only been able to win and retain political office by abandoning the substance of social democratic politics and (more or less shame-facedly) adopting the social and economic policies (and outcomes) favoured by their opponents.

The 'end of the Keynesian interlude' (if not always judgements about its consequences) is fairly common ground, even among those who would resist the latest bout of revisionism (see Hay, 1999, p. 71). But such a usage conceals as much as it reveals. Whether or not what went on in the 1950s and 1960s was properly called 'Keynesianism', the policy 'reversal' that took place from the mid-1970s was clearly stronger in Anglo-Saxon countries than elsewhere. The more successful and inclusive social democracies (generally elsewhere) were always aware of the importance of strategies that addressed the supply side of the economy (for both capital and labour). In any case, it really is not clear that 'classical' social democratic regimes were especially 'Keynesian' (and certainly not they alone, and, just as surely, to very differing degrees). Garrett (1998, p. 97) suggests that in the 'golden age' of social democracy (an epoch which virtually every rendering of this story evokes in one form or another and in which social democratic Keynesianism should have been at its peak) left governments often ran lower public budget deficits and tighter monetary policy than others. As to the welfare state element in the KWS, it is now something of an orthodoxy among students of social policy that welfare state institutions have been remarkably robust through the last twenty-five years of unremitting crisis (P. Pierson, 1998; C. Pierson, 1998a).

At the same time, social democrats are likely to be encouraged by the spectre of a revival in those approaches sometimes styled the 'new Keynesianism'. In fact, we should probably describe this revival of Keynesian thinking not so much as *new* but rather as *chastened*. Like its more self-confident forerunner, it relies on the invocation of Keynes not for some very specific and technical insight but rather for the general supposition that contemporary economies are subject to multiple forms of market failure *and* that something (but not quite everything that was once supposed) can be done about it. This renewal has already worked its way into the world of textbook macroeconomics but is still relatively neglected by political scientists, many of whom must be supposed not really to have come to terms with what Keynesianism meant the first time around (see Snowdon and Vane, 1997).

New Keynesianism is an 'approach' rather than a paradigm but it almost uniformly means abandoning some (rather cavalier) assumptions which are seen to have undermined the practice of an earlier generation. So, for example, it is often argued by the newer Keynesians that their classical forerunners erred in their beliefs about the trade-off between unemployment and inflation, in downgrading monetary policy, and in overestimating the capacity of governments to fine-tune the economy in the short term. But, so it is insisted, Keynesians were and are right to believe that market economies are vulnerable to chronic forms of market failure *and* that there are forms of intervention which governments (and others) may make which will ameliorate (though never eliminate) these problems.

This expectation elides, in turn, with a growing interest in the dynamics of growth (and what governments may do to support it). Social democratic politics has always been centrally concerned with questions of economic growth. For social democrats, securing the maximum possible levels of employment, improving social provision and finding forms of compromise with private investors has always been premised on a growing social product. The newer generation of writing on economic growth stresses the *endogenous* aspects of growth *and* the part that governments may play in sponsoring this process. Governments wishing to foster growth cannot do so (as once they may have imagined) by taking enterprises into public ownership or 'picking winners', but they can establish the *general* parameters and environment within which growth will be encouraged.

Within such a framework it is possible to read the centre-left's concern with an employment-based social policy not as a continuation of a preceding and neoliberal strategy to enforce the wage discipline of a deregulated labour market but rather as an attempt to enhance skills and adaptability in the interests of those who sell their labour power. In the virtuous reading of this process, it is about increasing the overall social product and maximizing the opportunities for individuals, exercising their skills and exploiting their adaptability, to maximize welfare for themselves and their families. I return to the possibilities this offers for a 'supply-side social democracy' a little later in this chapter.

(2) Social democracy remains committed to a leading role for the state and the public sector Traditionally, social democrats are seen to be committed to a 'big' and directive state and to an extensive public sector. Two arguments are now taken to weigh decisively against this extended social democratic state: first, that globalization is undermining the capacity of the interventionist (and revenue-raising) state and, secondly, that under conditions of reflexive modernity, states and their administrative methods are no longer effective in meeting the welfare needs (and expectations) of their populations. Under these circumstances, building up a workforce (and a constituency) in an extended public sector is countermanded by the need to increase productivity in the (public) service sector and, more generally, to meet the imperatives of international competitiveness. The challenge of demographic change can only be met by transferring more responsibility from states to markets and/or individuals and/or the 'third sector'.

This view of social democracy draws on considerable historical and comparative experience. Social democratic forces (though not they alone) have been intimately involved in the remarkable growth of state institutions throughout the twentieth century. Often social democrats have seen a special virtue in public provision of goods and services, sometimes tying this to conceptions of good citizenship. The 'most' social democratic states (above all, those in Scandinavia) have had a large public sector (though not always, it is worth noting, the most extensive public ownership) and Social Democratic parties have come to rely for their support on a constituency in the public sector, perhaps even more than in the traditional working class (see Kitschelt, 1994).

Nonetheless, the extent to which social democratic 'stateness' is unique is clearly overplayed. While those states in which social democracy has been an important force can be linked to the growth of government in the postwar period, the association is not straightforward. Partisan identity may have as much or more to do with the nature of government expenditures (transfers or public investment) as with their size (Esping-Andersen, 1990). There is a strong and non-partisan association between growth in the size of the state and demographic change, above all ageing – and this is unsurprising given what we know about the importance of social expenditure in total government outlays and the association between ageing and the scale of the public welfare effort (see Castles, 1998). It is certainly true that Social Democratic parties have generally been less enthusiastic about transferring activities and assets into the private sector, but some centre-left parties (notably the Australian Labor Party) have been in the vanguard of microeconomic change and (private) pension reform (P. Kelly, 1992; C. Pierson, 1998b). In any case, some of the most social democratic states (on most criteria) have had the lowest levels of public ownership.

At the same time, we need to recognize that the so-called 'new' social policy agenda does not anticipate a wholesale withdrawal of the state. States may become smaller (especially if a large part of their pensions effort is transferred to individuals) but in other areas (policing the labour market or the state-created health-care market, for example) the state becomes more intrusive and interventionist. As the state's direct delivery of services declines, so its *regulatory* function looks set to increase. We need to remember as well that it is a part of the historical compromise on which social democracy is based that it leaves the essential task of making a prosperous society to the initiative of private investors. Social democrats have always anticipated that the primary source of income for most citizens will be a product of their engagement in labour markets. Rarely have social democrats argued (in earnest) that the proper role of the state is to own and manage the 'commanding heights' of the economy. The 'end of the nation-state' has been much spoken of, but it has yet really to register in the accounts of national revenues and expenditures.

(3) Social democracy remains committed to an (unsustainable) strategy of high and progressive taxes Historically, social democrats have been identified with a commitment to the most

extensive and generous basis for social expenditure (in relation to pensions among other provisions). Generally, they have held that the burden of taxation should fall most heavily on those with the greatest capacity to pay. We have seen it argued that such a commitment is unsustainable in the light of current demographic developments, requiring a level of taxation of the incomes of future working populations which will be regarded as confiscatory. Democratic publics will not accept these levels of taxation, which would, in any case, grossly distort decisions to undertake waged work (in the formal economy, at least) or to invest capital, thus further lowering the levels of economic activity on which public consumption would depend. The capacity for revenue raising is also seriously compromised by the heightened international mobility of capital and (skilled) labour. The only viable strategy for the future is to reduce levels of social expenditure (above all, by restricting spending on transfers, including pensions) while constraining government revenues and making tax regimes less progressive. This is just the opposite of what 'classical' social democrats have sought to do (that is, increasing social expenditure and making taxation regimes more progressive).

It is true that social democratic regimes have often been associated with high levels of social expenditure and correspondingly high levels of government revenues. (Around 1995, the overall tax takes in Japan and the US were little more than half the figures for Denmark and Sweden). And there is some evidence that, in the 1990s, social democratic regimes (most notoriously in Sweden) had increasing difficulty in matching expenditure to income, leading to substantial public budget deficits (Castles, 1998, p. 120; Garrett, 1998, pp. 17, 137). Yet we need to bear in mind that all this was in a context in which the overall proportion of national product taken by governments everywhere in the developed world had risen substantially, even in the period after 1974. The 1990s saw some important changes in the tax base, as even the more social democratic regimes sought to reduce taxes on corporations and employers' social security contributions, transferring revenue-raising effort to taxes on consumption. However, these changes still left a range of quite distinctive tax regimes and, in fact, these tax reforms were frequently designed to be revenue neutral (with a flattening of schedules coupled to a widening of bases). In some cases, reductions in rates of corporation tax were offset by the removal of investment incentives for companies (see Swank, 1998a, 1998b). Social democratic regimes still had distinctive character-istics in both tax raising and public expenditure but they were far from uniformly the worst offenders in terms of accumulated public debt (Garrett, 1998, p. 138). The more successful social democratic regimes certainly have higher levels of taxation, but then they also provide manifestly better levels of public services for which their publics remain willing to foot the bill.

Despite the expectation that globalization would irresistibly drive taxes continuously, even precipitously, downwards, govern-ments have shown a considerable capacity to maintain their incomes and some success in protecting the most vulnerable from the shift towards indirect taxes (by exempting some essentials from goods and services taxes, for example). Generally, social democratic (and other) governments have moderated the progres-sivity of their taxes and shifted some of the burden away from taxes on employment, but without seeing a catastrophic decline in their incomes. Some regimes have moved in the direction of mandating individuals to contribute to their own private pension funds with an underpinning governmental apparatus of regulation and assistance for the lowest earners (for details of the Australian experience, see C. Pierson, 1998b). It is still the case, as Carles Boix argues (1998), that high taxes (and social security contribu-tions) may not frighten off investors *if* productivity (and rates of return) are sufficiently high and reliable.

(4) Social democracy remains committed to the goal of full employ-ment but opposes the very policy reforms that can maximize employability   Full employment has been an important aspiration of classical social democrats at least since the 1930s and it is one of the few policies explicitly enshrined in social democracy's principal international 'mission statement', the *Declaration of Principles* of the Socialist International (1999) – though without any very readily apparent machinery for its delivery. Certainly, those who heap praise on the great American jobs machine and contrast its success with double-digit unemployment in sclerotic European welfare states suggest that social democratic strategies are no longer consonant with maximum employability (though critics are also inclined to draw attention to the great job-creating

initiative represented by the United States penitentiary). Of course, the traditional social democratic aspiration was not just to see full employment but to see this in turn strengthen the bargaining position of labour, do away with the 'working (but) poor' and enable workers to fund their own welfare provision (through a mixture of taxes and earmarked social security contributions). The aspiration to maximize (any sort of) employment will hardly have the required effect in the wider economy if too many of the new workers are subsidized by a low earnings tax credit. Maximizing employment by reducing wages and conditions will not immediately recommend itself to social democratic forces – but it may not even present a 'solution' to the challenge posed by demographic ageing. The World Bank's aspiration to have (nearly) everyone pay for their own pension will not really work where significant numbers of workers cannot afford to make *any* savings for their retirement.

This may not, though, be the only road to an improved performance in terms of employability. Historically, it is those societies with the most entrenched labour market institutions or 'social dialogue' (not all of them social democratic) that have been best able to reconcile 'full employment' with 'competitiveness' (see Coates, 2000). Although its social democratic credentials may be in doubt (and its recent jobs performance not quite a 'miracle'), the Netherlands provides an alternative example of centrally coordinated growth in employment (Visser, 1998; de Beus, 1999). In essence, Dutch unions have traded an increase in jobs for wage moderation and a proliferation of part-time work. One million new jobs were added (to the existing 5 million) between 1985 and 1995. But nine out of ten of these recently created jobs have been part-time, leading to a situation in which more than one-third of the national workforce are in part-time employment (the highest average in the OECD). Unit labour costs have fallen, while wages have (just about) tracked price inflation (Visser, 1998). This has gone along with reforms of the social security system (tightening eligibility for early retirement and disability benefits) plus the introduction of a number of innovative labour market programmes. There is plenty of downside to the Dutch experience (including the persistence of long-term unemployment and the particular difficulties experienced by unskilled and immigrant workers), but it does show the potential for an alternative route to achieving American levels of job creation by other means (and without the attendant phenomenon of a mass of the working poor). (On the contrast between the Netherlands and the US, see also Goodin et al., 1999.)

(5) Social democratic conceptions of welfare are married to an unsustainable notion of social citizenship Citizenship (including social citizenship) has certainly featured significantly in social democratic discourse (see, for example, Esping-Andersen, 1990). It was an important component of the general social democratic supposition that the securing of parliamentary democracy under universal suffrage made (nearly) every adult a citizen. For many social democrats, it was an important element in the 'break-out' from a strictly workerist constituency. Citizenship described membership of a political community and, in Marshall's classic formulation of 1949, a network of rights embracing 'the whole range from the right to a modicum of economic welfare and security to the right to share to the full in the social heritage and to live the life of a civilised being according to the standards prevailing in the society' (Marshall, 1963, p. 74). A part of what was important about citizenship was that its rights did *not* depend on a person's economic status. To this extent, it is seen to be inconsistent with contemporary calls for an 'employment-based social policy'.

Yet the idea that social democratic conceptions of citizenship ever underwrote unconditional access for citizens to extensive societal resources is some way wide of the mark. In its most 'classical' form, in the writings of Bernstein (1909) or of T. H. Marshall (in 1949) for example, there is always an emphasis on both social rights *and* duties. This is an even-handedness which Giddens claims has now fallen into disuse and which he seeks to revive (although with the important qualification that citizenship is now confined to civil and political rights; see Giddens, 1998, p. 102). In practice, social democratic welfare policy was always a little more conditional than talk of citizenship rights might seem to suggest. In most welfare states, statutory entitlement was usually reserved for those who met the contributions or other criteria (being a veteran, for example), with a more discretionary system for those who lacked these qualifications. The end of full employment increased the numbers of those reliant on non-contributory benefits, but it did not create this category. It is clear why 'workfare' (work for benefits) should be seen generally (though not universally) as a breach of social democratic conceptions of an entitlement to compensation for unemployment, but the institution of an 'availability for work' test (however stringently or leniently applied) is not new. In fact, the idea that one might choose voluntary unemployment and still be supported by the state is quite at odds with the social democratic tradition (even though, as we shall see a little later, it is advocated now by the supporters of a Basic Income as a reasonable way to secure efficiency and social justice under changing social and economic circumstances).

In general, the idea that a citizens' welfare state meant largesse for whoever wanted it, with the costs deferred to future generations through the magic of a mushrooming public debt, is a story that is rather poorly supported by the available evidence (Garrett, 1998). Certainly, it is a part of the newer social policy agenda to increase discretion (for the state) and to transfer responsibilities away from public agencies and towards individuals and corporations. It is possible to trace a corresponding downplaying of the idea of citizenship in favour of self-reliance. But it is extremely difficult in a large-scale and complex society to step back entirely from a framework grounded in statutory entitlements and obligations. Indeed, citizens themselves are unlikely to respond positively to a regime in which it appears that everything is discretionary except their obligation to pay taxes.

(6) Social democracy is the politics of the labour movement: the decline of trade unions leaves social democracy ineffective and without a distinctive political purpose   That labour movements and the traditional class structure on which they were built have been in long-term decline and that these changes have led in their turn to a potentially disastrous loss of support and purpose for social democratic parties is an argument that came into its own in the 1980s and 1990s but, in fact, it has a history running all the way back to the 1950s (Abrams and Rose, 1960; Jenkins, 1987; Piven, 1992). The revival of social democratic electoral fortunes in the second half of the 1990s has caused only the mildest embarrassment to its critics, who now characteristically recast their argument to say that Social Democratic parties may get themselves elected but only by running on the platform of their opponents

(for a review, see C. Pierson, 1995). And no sooner had the rubric of corporatism become firmly established in the literature than it too was being recast as part of 'the world we have lost' (for critical surveys, see Rhodes 1998; Coates, 2000). These arguments feed off some real and substantial changes. Although social democratic parties were not generally, as in the UK, formally the product of trade union organization, almost everywhere the relationship between unions and social democratic parties has been crucial. And having peaked (in many instances as late as the 1980s), union densities have generally been in decline in recent years, though with some evidence that the pace of decline, at least, may be lessening (Golden, Wallerstein and Lange, 1999). Kitschelt (1994) is among those who have argued that this decline of unions and of the party–union link may actually be to the advantage of Social Democratic parties, who are then freer to reposition themselves in terms of an electorate with new interests and affiliations. But generally the expectation has been that the declining number of blue-collar workers will feed into declining numbers of trade unionists, leading to an important loss of institutional support and voter numbers for parties of the centre-left.

In fact, the story is a little less straightforward. Although there has been a general decrease in the numbers of unionized workers, this has not been uniform across states (with particularly precipitous falls in the US, the UK and Austria). As has been widely reported, unionization has tended to be strongest, and certainly the growth over the last twenty years principally concentrated, in the public sector and often among professional and clerical workers. At the same time, some national union organizations have been able 'to punch above their weight' because of longstanding relationships with organized capital and the state, or because of their privileged status (for example, in the management of unemployment funds or in the negotiation of sector-wide wage deals). Furthermore, there is just no straightforward correlation between declining union densities and support for Social Democratic parties.

Nor is the decline of corporatism quite so clear-cut. Rhodes (1998) is among those who have seen less a decline than a reorientation of corporatism in the 1990s. Thus he holds out the prospect of a 'competitive corporatism' in which the social partners continue to negotiate but now in a less favourable climate of social decrementalism focused on the underpinning of internationally competitive labour market regimes. In some instances (Australia is a good example) this made the relationship between unions and party *more* explicit in the 1980s and 1990s (on the Accord process, see Kelly, 1992). Even if corporatism is thought to have declined, it seems clear (Soskice, 1999) that differences in the 'successor regimes', based on the long-term institutional infrastructures of coordinated market economies (CMEs) and liberal market economies (LMEs), mean that the possibility of managing labour (and other) market outcomes will still be much easier in some (coordinated) polities than others.

Furthermore, as Esping-Andersen was one of the first to point out (1985), social democracy (as movement and party) has, in fact, always rested on the politics of class alliance. A 'pure' workers party could never succeed (electorally) in a developed industrial economy (Przeworski, 1985). To this extent, it has always sought support beyond the 'core' of the working class. At the same time, social democracy's commitment to the public sector and the welfare state has helped it to forge a strong constituency in the state-employed middle classes (whether unionized or not). Finally, Boix (1998) has argued that social democratic parties (and programmes) may flourish even *without* the support of a strong trade union movement. Indeed, he argues that (in the instance of Spain in the 1980s), the PSOE government ran a *more* redistributive social democratic programme in the absence of (perhaps even because of the absence of) effective institutional support in a corporatist trade union movement.

(7) A core ambition of social democrats is to alter the distribution of wealth and to generate less inequality (not just of 'opportunities' but also of outcomes); such ambitions are irreconcilable with the sorts of economic and social policies which competitiveness and growth require For many this will seem to be the key argument against the continuing integrity of social democratic politics. Social democracy has always been centrally concerned with the politics of redistribution. There has been a more or less consistent expectation (all the way back to Bernstein) that social democrats would use the agencies of the state under the authority of parliamentary democracy to effect a better outcome for their core constituency

among workers. Generally, social democrats have been confident in the real (but qualified) capacity of state institutions to deliver on this agenda, and sometimes this approach has been glossed as the logic of 'politics against markets' (Esping-Andersen, 1985; Korpi, 1979, 1983). Of course, all states (however small) redistribute, and all modern states redistribute extensively (though not always very progressively). Social democratic states therefore differ in degree and perhaps in purpose but not in kind from other forms of the modern state. Nor have social democrats always sought to redistribute from capital to labour or from rich to poor. Redistribution has often been in favour of children, the elderly and the infirm (the principal beneficiaries of welfare states) or across the life-cycle of workers either individually or collectively.

This proviso notwithstanding, social democrats have sought a narrowing of wealth differentials. They have sought a pattern in which incomes are less unequal. They have also sought to extend equality of both opportunity and outcome.[1] This is a process sometimes caricatured as 'tax and spend', but although social democrats have characteristically been big spenders (though not the only ones), they have just as often sought to realize their policy ambitions by other means. They have always accepted the existence of labour markets (though they have sought to regulate these more or less rigorously) and have seen growth in wages (and economic growth more generally) as a principal mechanism in achieving their desired outcomes. The business of reconciling a desire for increased equality of income with the dynamics of an economy that remains substantially beholden to the decisions of private investors has always been tricky.

It is hard not to think that there was a time when this trick was easier to finesse. A rapidly growing national product, full employment and a seemingly greater willingness to accept the authority of governmental decisions (very roughly the circumstances of the 1950s and 1960s) gave plenty of leeway for the practitioners of a social democratic politics. Current circumstances (sluggish growth, widespread unemployment, the pressure of demographic change and a seeming disenchantment with representative democracy) certainly make this much more difficult – but not necessarily impossible. Of course, there are plenty on both left and right who think that a social democratic option was never worth pursuing in the first place – for them, it can never be too soon for social democrats to relinquish their misguided ambitions. For those who, for whatever reason, continue to think that this is a politics worth pursuing, and given the poverty of all the available alternatives, it seems too soon to abandon all hope.

The Third Way?

Even for those who remain committed to a social democratic agenda, there is plenty of evidence in this volume that pursuing this politics 'in the old way' (even when we have stripped out all the misrepresentation that goes with this characterization) is just not possible. Given this, how should we set about the 'refurbishment' or 'renewal' of social democracy? And, initially and more specifically, what if any part should be played in this process by much-heralded visions of a 'third way'?

If there is a new vista opening up for social democrats, this could hardly be described as a first journey down the third way. The quest for something that is not-quite-capitalism and not-quite-socialism is more than a hundred years old. Indeed, for much of the twentieth century social democracy was itself synonymous with the attempt to steer a middle course between what was seen as the deformed and authoritarian socialism of the Soviet Union and the rapacious dog-eat-dog capitalism of the United States (see, for example, Childs, 1947). Between, or (in the preferred usage of its advocates) beyond, which two models the newest third way is supposed to chart a course remains unclear. In chapter 1 (see pp. 12–14 above), we saw that Giddens styles the third way 'an attempt to transcend both old-style social democracy and neoliberalism'. Elsewhere, he describes it as 'social democratic politics after the end of socialism' or, still more simply, as 'modernized social democracy', and the latter usage more or less coincides with Tony Blair's own account in his 1998 Fabian pamphlet (Giddens, 1998, 1999; Blair, 1998, p. 1). As Giddens acknowledges (2000, pp. 2–4), the inspiration for this vision of the third way lies principally with the New Progressivism adopted by Bill Clinton (whose restoration of Democrat fortunes was much admired among Labour Party modernizers in

the early 1990s). In Clinton's account, the third way defines a
trajectory above and beyond the beliefs and expectations of those
who saw government respectively as either 'the problem' or 'the
answer'. It was an alternative to 'the liberal impulse to defend
the bureaucratic status quo and the conservative bid to simply
dismantle government' (Progressive Foundation, 1996). Given
these origins, the fashioning of a third way appears to owe little
to what has passed for social democratic thought in Britain and
still less to the traditions of the reformist left in continental and
northern Europe (see Giddens, 2000; Gamble and Wright, 1999).

The core values of the third way are identified by the New
Progressives as 'equal opportunity, mutual responsibility and self-
governing citizens and communities' (Progressive Foundation,
1996, p. 27). These ideas are fleshed out in Stuart White's careful
(if brief) contribution to the 1998 *Nexus* online debate (White,
1998a). In White's account, the third way occupies a 'relatively
large' and contested conceptual space, rather than defining a
single programme. Within this space, he identifies three common
features. First, there is an emphasis on 'real opportunity' (to be
distinguished from its neoliberal predecessor by the supposition
that the state and the community have some responsibility to
ensure that individuals are equipped with the resources and skills
that enable them to exploit a structure of opportunities). Secondly, there is a concern with civic responsibility. The decline in
a sense of civic responsibility (matching rights with duties) is seen
to have been one of the vices of 'traditional' social democracy,
although the idea of rights and duties of citizenship is retraced to
the founding figures of welfare state social democracy (to Marshall and Hobhouse, for example). Responsibility does not mean,
though – as it is supposed it did for neoliberals – complete self-
reliance (and the sense that, having claimed their rights and
attended to their duties, individuals need have no further interaction with the wider society). This leads into the third element
that White finds to be characteristic of third way thinking: an
emphasis on the idea of community. At one time it was this that
seemed most distinctive and innovative in the Blairite account of
a new politics. It was certainly argued that this sense of community marked out a New Labour politics (which could still be
tough in areas such as crime and welfare) from what were
depicted as its twin predecessors: the corrosive selfishness of

Thatcherism and the sentimental, imaginary and exclusionary Merrie England ('warm beer and cricket on the village green') of John Major.

Alongside these general characteristics of third way thinking, five programmatic realignments can be derived from White (1998a):

- the regulatory (rather than the provider) state;
- the advocacy of 'mutualism' (i.e. collective forms of provision outside, but possibly underwritten by, the state);
- tax reform (new forms and retargeting);
- an employment-centred social policy;
- 'asset-based egalitarianism' (addressing issues of inequality through equipping citizens with social capital/skills/education rather than through the redistribution of resources).

Third way: new politics or old excuses?

The politics of the third way has a peculiarly Anglophone provenance (however universally it may be recommended).[2] In some ways, this is strange. At first sight, Britain, the US and Australia (along with New Zealand and Canada) look like the *least* plausible candidates in refashioning a social democratic politics. After all, Britain might be thought to have had one of the *least* successful social democratic movements of the twentieth century, Australia one of the most idiosyncratic and the US one of the most invisible. Meanwhile, 'new' social democratic thinking in continental Europe (the *Neue Mitte* in Germany, the *Polder* model in Holland, still more *la gauche plurielle* in France) looks rather different (see G. Kelly, 1999). Under these circumstances, it is perhaps unsurprising that Scandinavians (and some continental Europeans) have asked why they should look to the Anglo-American experience for guidance given that 'these countries are not welfare states in any sense that is familiar and accepted by most people in the Nordic countries' (cited in Giddens, 2000, pp. 16–17; see also Jospin, 1999).

In Britain, though, 'the third way' has become the near-universal currency – sometimes a term of affection, often of contempt and somewhat infrequently of analysis – in which to evaluate the 'new politics'. As such, it has been hotly contested but consistently underspecified. There are certainly plenty of critics willing to dismiss advocacy of the third way as an exercise designed to mask the fact that the new politics of the centre-left will mean 'business as usual' (see, *inter alia*, Hay, 1999; Coates, 2000). Certainly we might wonder if the idea of a third way so readily and seamlessly replaced 'stakeholding' (the 'big idea' that briefly preceded it) because the latter represented a *really* clear and radical break with what had gone before. But it is still perhaps a little too harsh to dismiss the third way as nothing more than a skilful rebranding of some tried and mistrusted neoliberal ideas. Its critique of an older social democratic tradition may be misleading and the continuity with what has gone before is clear enough. But it does take at least one step back from some of the wilder outposts of the New Right. Although Giddens is widely criticized (perhaps rightly) for having given an especially conservative reading of third way politics, even he seems unambiguously committed to the continuing need for social democrats to redistribute (although what they should redistribute is a little less clear).

The third way does then afford some policy space for those who wish to moderate the outcomes that more committed neoliberals might welcome. If we consider the Australian experience (widely canvassed as a source for Blairite reforms), we see that alongside those critics who saw Hawke and Keating as the neoliberal betrayers of Australian labour are defenders of the ALP's conduct as a pragmatic 'refurbishment' of the Australian model of social protection under rapidly changing internal and external circumstances (see C. Pierson, 2000). For its critics (Wiseman, 1996, for example), of course, advocacy of 'progressive competitiveness' offers little more than 'a kinder road to hell'. For others, the politics of the third way looks like a classical (and not necessarily unworthy) exercise in reformist statecraft: accommodating to what are perceived to be unshiftable limits to policy-making, making the best of a bad job – and saying that it was what one wanted to do anyway.

The third way might then sometimes merit our qualified support, but where it is simply the rubric for giving up on elements of a social democratic politics which are still doable (if difficult), we should resist it. Many of the reforms that Giddens recommends on the basis of his influential reading of the third way, and which were discussed in chapter 1, seem to me to fall into this category. Critics are right here, I think, to charge Giddens with conceding too much to neoliberal prejudice where a little empirical social science (*pace* Garrett, 1998; Castles, 1998) would show that these views (especially on the nature of the welfare state) are quite unfounded. Certainly it would seem perverse to seek to export to societies with a much more vigorous and successful social democratic tradition approaches which have been fashioned out of the *weaknesses* of Anglophone experience.

In the end, the label is not so important (though it could be politically consequential). The issue is not under what name we should proceed but what kind of answer we have to Stuart White's question: 'What kind of institutions would enable us to have, simultaneously, an efficient, dynamic market economy, and a distribution of resources that is just in egalitarian terms (and I mean egalitarian, not merely "meritocratic")?' (White, 1998b). 'Third way thinking' provides one partial set of answers, but there are others – and it is to some of these that I turn in the remaining sections of this chapter.

Renovating social justice

One answer to White's question is to say that we need to update, refurbish or renovate (traditional) social democracy to bring its institutional framework in line with recent social and economic change. Just such a response, provided in some detail, can be found in the 1994 report of the Commission on Social Justice established by the then leader of the British Labour Party, John Smith (Commission on Social Justice, 1994). The remit of the commission was to consider how what was taken to be the traditional social democratic aspiration to promote social justice could be reconciled with a series of profound changes in economy and society. Although it lacked the cachet of a single 'big idea', the commission did benefit from the input of a number of economists and people with an expertise in the 'nuts and bolts' of social policy. Its final report was shaped by this expertise and included a number of fairly specific policy recommendations, many of which have found their way (if sometimes a little bastardized) into subsequent New Labour practice (although others have apparently sunk without trace). It was self-consciously presented as a renovation of social democratic principles under changing circumstances rather than as the attempt to forge an alternative – though perhaps inevitably, it placed its emphasis upon social 'investment' between and beyond 'deregulation' and 'levelling' (Commission on Social Justice, 1994, pp. 95–6).

Rather unfashionably, the report proceeded from a normative consideration of what should count as social justice. In addition to the standard liberties associated with a liberal democratic order, the report insisted that, 'as a right of citizenship' and reflecting 'a substantive commitment to the equal worth of all citizens', everyone is entitled 'to be able to meet their basic needs for income, shelter and other necessities'. They are also entitled to 'opportunities and life chances' (and this was said to explain why the commission was 'concerned with the primary distribution of opportunity, as well as redistribution'). Furthermore, while not all inequalities are unjust, 'unjust inequalities should be reduced and where possible eliminated' (1994, p. 18). These principles left members of the commission with very considerable discretion, but they did at least lay down some guidelines in terms of both citizenship and social justice.

The main body of the report identified a series of 'revolutionary' changes (a mix by now familiar of globalization, changes in the status and working lives of women and a changing relationship between citizen and state) that have rendered the tried and trusted social democratic routes to social justice impassable. A new social democratic order could only be built on 'a new combination of active welfare state, reformed labour market, and strong community' (p. 96). Combining the 'ethics of community' with the 'dynamics of a market economy', the report insisted that 'the extension of economic opportunity is not only the source of economic prosperity but also the basis of social justice': 'The competitive requirement for constant innovation and higher quality demands opportunities for every individual . . . to contribute to national economic renewal; this in turn demands strong social institutions, strong families and strong communities' (p. 95).

At the heart of the report's concerns are lifelong education and employment. Echoing calls for an 'active' society, the commission insisted that the privileged road to social justice lay not through

redistribution but through providing a framework of opportunities which individuals, empowered by new skills and compe-
tencies, would be able to exploit. The aspiration is to sponsor a
virtuous marriage between efficient production and just distribution (of both wealth and opportunities), maximizing the production of wealth through developing a highly skilled and adaptable
workforce. The role of government in securing social justice is
still seen to be extensive, indeed in some areas expanding, but
this is not primarily about the redistribution of resources through
taxes and benefits (this is what the report styles the 'Levellers'
agenda). The principal duties of a modern social democratic state
are to promote lifelong learning (raising levels of human capital),
to support 'full employment in a modern economy' (not by itself
creating jobs but through promoting employability) and to underpin social security.

For most people the principal route into economic and social
security will be through work, but this cannot be achieved,
certainly cannot be achieved consistent with the expectations of
social justice, simply by deregulating labour markets. Labour
markets need to be 'flexible' but in a context where the state
helps to create new pathways from 'welfare to work' and also
provides new forms of security for workers exposed to greater
uncertainty. It also involves a new gendered settlement in which
there is a reallocation of opportunities and responsibilities
between men and women in both paid and unpaid work. Upon
this account, states cannot defy changes in the international or
global economy, nor can they countermand the impact of new
technologies. But in accepting greater flexibility (and the need for
new and renewable skills), the state can assist its population. The
proposals for enhancing employability are not then solely about
deregulation. They are also, for example, about introducing
unemployment benefits geared to the growing numbers of part-
time workers and the self-employed and providing an infrastructure of childcare to enable single mothers to participate in the
paid workforce. For retired people, the commission recommended a universal second pension and a new minimum pension
guarantee, balancing some targeting of resources for the elderly
against a continuing commitment to an extensive public role.

It is clear that the sort of agenda established by the Commission shares many premises with the advocates of a third way. Its

account of the ways in which the world has changed to render pre-existing social democratic strategies outdated is broadly the same. It shares the emphasis on an employment-centred social policy and an 'asset-based egalitarianism'. There is also some continuity in the sorts of proposals it recommends (for example, in the emphasis on raising the quality of human capital and encouraging a movement from 'welfare to work'). But it is important to see that there are also some very real differences in the two approaches. The commission has much less sympathy with neoliberal criticisms of the welfare state (which is over-whelmed not so much by its own contradictions as by a changing external environment). It sees a much more extensive and positive continuing role for that state (although it wants to make plenty of space for voluntary, mutual and individual initiative too). It defends the continuing integrity of social insurance over against the claimed superiority of private solutions. It defends (a qualified) universalism against the insistence that welfare services must increasingly be targeted on the 'needy'. There is something of a paradox here. The sociology of the third way is more radical and provocative than the story of profound but incremental change that underpins the commission's proposals. But it is the third way that ends up substantively much closer to the 'new orthodoxy' of the World Bank and the OECD. This combination of radical premises and conservative conclusions may be a part of its appeal.

The case for a basic income

For a *really* radical approach to both the premises of *and* the solution to current social democratic dilemmas, we should turn to the arguments of the advocates of a basic income. For them, securing the core values of social democracy is now possible only through a series of radical institutional reforms that abandon much of the traditional terrain of social democratic politics. The postwar welfare state settlements were largely successful in achieving the great social democratic ambition of joining social justice to economic efficiency (while protecting individual free-dom). But this union has become increasingly dysfunctional and it is necessary now to move forward towards a 'second marriage of justice and efficiency' built around the introduction of a basic income (BI).

The core initiative is to introduce for all citizens an unconditional basic income: 'A basic income . . . is an income paid by the government to each full member of society (1) even if she is not willing to work, (2) irrespective of being rich or poor, (3) whoever she lives with, and (4) no matter which part of the country she lives in' (van Parijs, 1995, p. 35). BI might be set at different levels for different categories of people (with rather more for the elderly and disabled, and a lower rate for children) but in essence it is unconditional in that it is paid to all residents/ citizens of a political community as individuals without any test of income or assets and irrespective of employment or household status and without any indication of a 'willingness to work'. The level of BI is an open question. It is certainly not intended to be 'basic' in the sense that it should meet some specified (minimum) set of basic needs. In fact, it could be set *below* subsistence level (and need to be 'topped up' by other sources of income), but it is clear that the aspiration of most of its supporters is that it should be set at a level which would allow it to replace all existing income maintenance benefits and allow for the abolition of all personal reliefs set against income tax (McKay, 1998). Van Parijs (1995) presents an argument for the BI to be set at the maximum feasible level.

Advocates of a BI solution begin from some of the same social and economic changes as did the Commission on Social Justice and the exponents of a third way. They too focus on the changed world of work, but draw quite opposite conclusions. The first marriage of justice and efficiency under postwar welfare state regimes was built around progressive taxation, full employment, corporatist industrial relations, massified semi-skilled labour, Fordist labour processes and constrained capital mobility. That world is gone. Where lifelong employment (and its attendant pensions and social insurance rights) are much less certain, where relations between men and women and between both and the world of formal employment are so changed, where marriage is increasingly a serial experience, the old remedies are increasingly unworkable. The key ambition of employment-oriented social policies is to seek to reproduce a political economy of full employment (though in an updated and gender-neutral way). But this is impossible. Jobs can only be created (with great difficulty) by 'flexibilization' – lowering wages and conditions – and stable careers, or, a little less grandly, steady employment from 16 to 64 (which made many aspects of social insurance work), seem to have disappeared. Those who are employed claim to have too much work, while those who cannot get a job have inadequate incomes. This is perverse. Technology has rendered much work redundant and the aspiration to grow our way to fuller employment comes up against real ecological limits. The problem is not a shortage of work but the relationship between employment and income. To secure the coupling of social justice to economic efficiency (and ecological sustainability) now means partially disengaging income from employment – and moving to the maximum sustainable Basic Income for all citizens.

Much of the discussion that has surrounded the case for a basic income has turned on the justification of an *unconditional* income and the suspicion that this would allow the idle to exploit those who choose to work (see, for example, White, 1997). Although this is an important debate, I am more interested here to explore those arguments with which advocates of BI defend their proposals as a way out of the contemporary dilemmas of social democracy. In the face of those who argue that with a BI no one would ever leave the beach, supporters insist that a maximal BI would actually prove to be economically efficient (as well as socially just). Critics insist that a BI set at even a quite modest level would undermine incentives, discouraging the less skilled from entering the labour market and placing a fiscal burden on capital and on more skilled workers which would encourage them to lessen their effort or withdraw from the formal economy altogether. Supporters of a BI are generally sanguine about these objections. At one level, they resist the idea that maximizing growth and employment are unqualified goods. Insisting that there is an ecological limit to 'justice through growth', they encourage us to think of solutions that would involve both working and consuming less. Philippe van Parijs (1995), for example, argues that what we should be seeking to maximize is not income but 'real freedom for all' (allowing individuals to choose as freely as possible what it is they want to do with their lives). Supporters of BI argue further that traditional accounts (and welfare states) have always privileged paid employment over other forms of work (especially the unpaid labour of women within the household), which have often been seen not to count as work at all. But even within a more traditional economic mode of accounting, BI is said to be efficient. It allows individuals to take on work at very low wages (because of the income support that BI would provide). It would allow workers to retrain without excessive cost, to start new enterprises without undue personal risk. It would encourage greater flexibility in forms of work and easier movement between household and employment. In general, a BI is said to deliver 'flexibility with security', a combination which 'completely overshadows' concerns about the disincentive effects of the new (and extensive) tax regime on which it would be based (van Parijs, 1992, p. 233).

Advocates of an unconditional BI have some powerful arguments on their side. Over the past twenty years the social democratic ambition to squeeze income differences has given way almost everywhere (though unevenly) to increasing economic inequality. A successful BI should not only reverse this trend. Set at a moderately high level, it would cut a swathe through the existing jungle of conditional benefits and entitlements (and its many anomalies) to leave a clear and unambiguous commitment to adequate baseline incomes for all. Its promise to unhitch the delivery of social justice from an unqualified commitment to economic growth should recommend it to those (like Tony Giddens) who perceive real ecological limits to traditional social democratic incrementalism. It also promises to make good on the commitment to deliver on substantive gender equality, where the social democratic record is at best uneven. The claim is that this programme of radical and egalitarian change can be delivered while maximizing individual freedom and without presenting an implausible challenge to the institutional apparatus of existing private-ownership market economies. This is, quite explicitly, a model for a basic income *capitalism* (van Parijs, 1995).

Despite these considerable strengths, there is good reason to doubt that in the foreseeable future the advocacy of BI is likely to recommend itself as the preferred solution of any major social democratic party confronting the issue of reform. Some doubt that the efficiency-enhancing side-effects of reform will actually work. Many persist in the belief that a truly unconditional BI can only function through the exploitation of those who choose to work. But perhaps the more important obstacles are more immediately political. First, most Social Democratic parties are at present committed to policies that take them in precisely the opposite direction, that is *intensifying* the connection between work and income in an effort to increase overall levels of employment. Secondly, a substantial BI will require a significantly increased tax burden. Whatever might be the benefits that this increased tax-take would generate, contemporary politicians are more or less universally persuaded that a platform which promises significant tax increases is electorally suicidal. Thirdly, there is an issue about where a BI might be introduced and the nature of its relationship to other (and more conventional) polities. Can there be BI capitalism in just one country or just one economic community and, if not, through what sort of political mechanism (and what enforcement agency) might it be introduced? The idea of a basic income (which has been around at least since Paine first floated the idea in the 1790s (Paine, 1985)) is unlikely to go away. Although the current conventional wisdom insists on tightening the relationship between employment and income, it is quite unclear that in the long run this is a strategy that will work. Still, in a context where most people believe that politics is about the serving of powerful interests rather than the promotion of an ethically optimal community, BI may struggle to get a fair hearing.

A supply-side social democracy?

If Basic Income is (for now, at least) a little too radical to be able to win the support of mainstream Social Democratic parties, are there any other alternatives? In this section I want briefly to consider two strategic responses that go more with the flow of contemporary governing opinion but which still seek to stake out a distinctive space for a future social democratic politics. In chapter 3, we looked at the contested attempt to derive a 'new' social democratic model from the experience of the Australian Labor Party in the Hawke–Keating years (1983–96). What was interesting about the Australian experience was that through the 1980s and the first half of the 1990s the ALP had been responsible for a series of micro-economic reforms (including the floating of the Australian dollar and a series of high-profile privatizations) which elsewhere were identified with neoliberal forces. There was also an innovative pension reform which legislated a major transfer of liabilities into a private (but mandatory and highly regulated) savings regime. All of these reforms were carried through in a series of pacts or 'Accords' with the Australian Council of Trade Unions (ACTU). Defenders of the process saw in it an attempt to accommodate to an increasingly difficult external environment while protecting the most vulnerable domestic communities (a sort of social democracy of managed retreat). Critics saw in it a rather less principled politics of unqualified retreat.

In an instructive commentary, Herman Schwartz (1998, 2000a) has argued that the experience of Australia's Labor Party (especially when contrasted with the fate of its fellow party in New Zealand) may have a few strategic lessons for social democrats elsewhere, especially in Western Europe. The Australian labour movement has long faced the sorts of circumstances (of internationally mobile capital and debt-ridden states) which help to define the 'new' circumstances of European social democracy exposed to global economic forces. In Schwartz's view, the traditional strategies of the Australian labour movement were peculiarly well adapted to these circumstances of external economic vulnerability. Above all, they involved working with a smaller but more distributive social state and having a good deal of social protection delivered directly through the employment relationship, underpinned by a supportive judicial process. Historically, Australia secured a comparatively compressed income profile alongside a system of entrenched workplace rights without an extensive redistributive state (and with a correspondingly small tax-take). In circumstances where the 'big' welfare states with comparatively high levels of taxation and extensive social expenditure find their political and economic bases under threat, there is a suggestion that there may be useful lessons to be learnt from this antipodean experience. Indeed, Schwartz (2000) suggests that a part of Tony Blair's success in Britain may be directly attributed to his successful 'Australianization of Labor'.

But for all its strengths and interest, the Australian model may not travel well. Britain is perhaps much better placed for (and more kindly disposed towards) the adoption of Australian lessons.

These two countries share a good deal in terms of culture, legal forms and constitutional arrangements (as well as a head of state!). It seems clear that many European social democrats, including Lionel Jospin (1999), have very little intention of subscribing to this model of public sector reform. But even the parallel with the UK is limited. After all, a good deal of the ALP's success in the 1980s and 1990s was the product of the special relationship between the ACTU and the ALP, the nearly unique Australian system of awards wage setting and the capacity of ACTU to deliver on its side of the Accord bargain. Levels of trust and compliance between the ACTU and the ALP were similar to those that existed in the most successful days of Swedish party–union cooperation. This is almost unimaginable in a British (or indeed a French) context.

Radical social security reform may also be more difficult to effect in a European setting. Here the existence of social insurance means that many citizens will feel (perhaps rightly) that they have already made the necessary contributions to fund their existing entitlements (including pensions). In turn, this means that the problem of 'double pension payments' (involving a generation that must pay for the pensions of both its elders and itself) arises in a much more acute and politically problematic way in Europe. Introducing Australian forms and levels of means testing in Europe would be difficult not only for cultural and political reasons, but also because of their interaction with existing areas of social provision, poverty, employment traps and so on. In fact, with the further industrial relations reforms that have been implemented by Keating's Liberal-National successors (and with the ALP's formal abandonment of the Accord process), it may be that the Labor decade represented a 'window of opportunity' for reform. Path dependency and inertia may just about sustain the process in Australia – but even here (as rather earlier and more decisively in New Zealand) there is an issue about what happens to 'progressive competitiveness' once a more unambiguously market-oriented government is installed.

Finally, I want to turn to a more generic account of a distinctive supply-side social democracy which looks much more explicitly and directly to the European experience. Carles Boix's (1998) comparative study of the experience of the British Conservative Party and the Spanish Social Workers' Party (PSOE) during the

1980s is designed to give empirical substance to his theoretical claim that, if we live in an age where the supply side rules, there nonetheless remain very distinctive partisan strategies for managing the modern economy. There is a widely held belief, put rather briefly and crudely, that demand-side economic macro-management belonged to the social democrats and to the 1950s and 1960s, whereas supply-side macro-management is the natural terrain of more conservative parties and belongs to the 1980s, the 1990s (and beyond). Boix's move is to accept (broadly speaking) that politicians must now direct most of their attention to the supply side of the economy. But he insists that this does not mean that social democrats are permanently caught playing 'catch up' with neoliberal innovators. In fact, Boix argues that there are very distinctive, perhaps even increasingly distinctive, approaches to supply-side macro-management on left and right.

The essential insight (or prejudice) that underpins supply-side economic interventions is that 'overall economic performance is eventually a function of the level and the quality of the production factors – fixed capital and human capital.' But, in fact, there are 'two main alternative supply-side economic strategies . . . to maximise growth and ensure the international competitiveness of domestic firms': 'The first strategy consists in reducing taxes to encourage private savings, boost private investment, and accelerate the rate of growth . . . [Under] the second strategy . . . the state increases public spending in human and fixed capital to raise the productivity of labor and capital: *this should encourage private agents to keep investing even in the face of high taxation.*' Social democratic parties seek to establish 'a "virtuous circle" in which higher productivity continues to attract private capital but allows for higher wages and taxes, which are then used to sustain and increase higher productivity' (Boix, 1998, pp. 3, 30).

Far from globalization having forced a convergence in governing responses, Boix insists that it has 'on the contrary, magnified the role of (competing) supply-side economic strategies and intensified the importance of parties and partisan agency in the selection of policies' (1998, p. 4). For strategists of both right and left, there are electoral costs and opportunities in pursuing these diverging agenda. Clearly a social democratic 'public investment' strategy requires greater government revenues and this requires that a greater tax burden fall on capital and/or the middle classes.

To make this acceptable, social democrats must ensure first that the climate for investment is sufficiently good to attract capital despite taxation or non-wage labour costs and, secondly, that the level of public services is such that middle-class voters will not be tempted away by a right-wing alternative of low taxes and a low social wage. For social democrats, there is a further dilemma in reconciling their commitment to public *investment* (for example, in infrastructure and education) with calls for more extensive social *transfers* to its core constituency among society's least affluent. This presents a more acute electoral (rather than moral) problem when the poor both vote and have a left-of-centre alternative to which they can pledge their support.

At the same time, as Boix insists, partisan supply-side strategies also offer opportunities. The interests to which parties appeal are not fixed. They are in part constituted by the policies and performance of parties themselves. Where a party is able to sustain itself in power beyond a single term (especially where it can entrench itself for a decade or more) it can try to shape the sorts of communities of interest to which it must then make an electoral appeal. A simple example from an entrenched Conservative administration was the attempt by Margaret Thatcher to secure the support of skilled working-class voters through discounted council house sales and below-value privatizations.[3] At the same time, the fate of the British Conservatives shows just how volatile such 'new' allegiances can be (given that voters are systematically ungrateful for past favours).

It is not absolutely clear that Boix's evidence will bear the full weight of his theoretical assumptions. Although he shows powerful evidence of a partisan effect on levels of public investment, the claims of Thatcher to have forged a 'low-tax' regime are now widely contested. At least a part of the expansive spending experience under Gonzalez in Spain may be attributed to a process of democratic state-building after the Franco years. Similarly, the claim that social democratic regimes would take an increasingly divergent attitude to privatization (from their right-wing opponents) looks a little less secure at the start of the twenty-first century. Perhaps, as well, there is too much striving for effect in the arguments that these two strategies are exclusive and, under the impact of globalization, increasingly so. In a rather messy political practice, especially where social democrats find themselves in coalition with partners to both left and right, it is possible that policy on the ground will pick and mix between the preferred supply-side options of both right and left. Nonetheless, Boix's argument is a powerful corrective to those who see no scope for a social democratic politics (or indeed for parties more generally), and demonstrates that, within a very tight space, Social Democratic parties may not only make a difference but can seek across time to build up 'progressive' alliances which will strengthen the institutional underpinnings of their kind of supply-side macro-management.

Conclusion

Throughout this book, I have tried to show that those who advise us to abandon the rubric of a more 'traditional' social democracy have justified this appeal through a highly selective use of both historical and contemporary evidence. Looking back across a hundred years of political practice, these critics, represented here by Gray and Giddens, have used a highly stylized model of a single (if particularly important) strand in social democratic experience as the basis for a much more general questioning of its continued viability. Turning to the contemporary period, they have argued that the aspirations of social democrats (at least as these have been traditionally conceived) will inevitably be disappointed by the new context of demographic change and a globalized economy. Yet we have seen that social democracy is a much more diverse and resourceful tradition than this truncated history would suggest and many of these criticisms fall wide of their target.

Here I take just two examples. We saw above (p. 7) that John Gray has argued that 'the global freedom of capital effectively demolishes the economic foundations of social democracy' (Gray, 1996, p. 26). Yet the empirical evidence reviewed in chapter 4 reveals that this seemingly plausible claim just cannot be sustained. Similarly, Giddens argues in a number of places that welfare states have created as many problems as they have solved. In vindicating this sweeping judgement, Giddens invites us to take a good deal of the neoliberal case on work disincentives, dependency and the hazards of public provision at face value. But, once again, a more careful evaluation of the empirical evidence (some of which is cited in chapters 3 and 5 above) reveals a much more complex picture in which the assumptions of the neoliberal critics of social protection are really rather poorly supported. At the same time, the 'alternatives' that Gray and Giddens offer themselves lack an adequate account of political agency. Giddens, for example, talks of 'social pacts' between rich and poor (seemingly about everything other than the distribution of wealth – the *real* issue), but this is, in some sense, exactly what the 'old' and rejected forms of social democracy aimed to deliver. The corporatism of the small European social democracies was precisely about giving institutional effect to 'social pacts'. Welfare and wage settlements were the price that capital paid to labour not just for its work effort but for its acquiescence in a regime based on private property and markets (and market 'adjustments'). Only a little unfairly, the Gray–Giddens positions could be described as all politics and no agency (contrasting with a social democracy which has sometimes been seen to be all agency and no politics).

Thus, while contemporary changes certainly make life harder for social democrats (among others), their impact is much less dramatic than its critics have supposed. At the outset of the twenty-first century, social democracy is, if not quite kicking, at least very much alive. Yet, even for its supporters, this is not an entirely reassuring finding. If, as Gamble and Wright suppose, the rather modest core of the social democratic enterprise is the attempt 'to build and sustain political majorities for reforms of economic and social institutions which will counter injustice and reduce inequality' (1999, p. 2), it seems clear that this has become increasingly difficult. Indeed, it seems sometimes as if social democracy is the politics of perpetually diminishing expectations. In Perry Anderson's rhetorical formulation:

Once, in the founding years of the Second International, [social democracy] was dedicated to the general overthrow of capitalism. Then it pursued partial reforms as gradual steps towards socialism. Finally it settled for welfare and full employment within capitalism. If it now accepts a scaling down of the one and giving up the other, what kind of movement will it change into? (Anderson and Camiller, 1994, pp. 15–16)

One answer is that social democracy isn't really a social movement at all (any more). It is a part of the routinized 'normal' politics of affluent liberal democracies. Upon this view, the expectation (almost always disappointed) that social democracy should pursue a transformative social and political agenda is archaic, a prejudice left over from a more radical past (or at least from a history of more radical expectations). The mundane practice of Social Democratic parties is perhaps just not the right place to look for new ideas about the transformation of social and political life. It may be that social democracy's task is the no less noble, though certainly rather duller business of making life a little less awful for the most disadvantaged (the *comparatively* disadvantaged, that is, within the world's most affluent societies) and a little more secure for ordinary citizens. For busy politicians and policy-makers, this means very largely working with the institutions and resources that are already at hand. Yet this does not mean a politics which is solely defensive or an approach which is purely opportunistic (though who is it that wants to let a good opportunity go unexploited?). Whatever may be the structural limits that social democrats face, there always remains *some* scope for making a difference and, if we look back over the last hundred years, the cumulative impact of incremental change (despite occasional setbacks) is enormous (if always, in the eyes of its utopian critics, rather pitiful).

But if it is necessary to keep faith with a traditional social democratic programme of social amelioration, it is certainly not sufficient. Changing circumstances do pose a series of intractable problems for social democrats (though these are not always those which feature most prominently in the accounts of its contemporary critics). All these can be said to relate in some way to social democracy's tendency to be reactive (rather than proactive) and to its pragmatic eclecticism. First, despite all the changes that we have seen in recent years and the 'opening' to environmentalism (see Jacobs, 1999), social democracy remains married to the conviction that the key to managing distributional conflict is economic growth. (Despite his sensitivity to the limits to growth, Giddens fails to confront this issue effectively in his account of a 'modernized' social democracy.) This has generated some institutional or party political problems (especially where Social Democrats have sought to work in alliance with Greens), but it goes beyond this. Wherever the limits to economic growth lie, it seems clear that distributional conflict *cannot* be resolved indefinitely by substituting growth for redistribution. What is at issue here is not just the environmental limits to growth (vital as these must be) but also the sense that the benefits of maximizing economic activity (one might almost say, at any cost) may be outweighed by the losses for individual well-being. Do we, for example, still value 'full employment' even if the price is growing wage dispersion, declining terms and conditions for those with the fewest marketable skills and an end of effective representation in the workplace? In the face of the recent barrage of micro-economic reforms, we really need (and presently lack) the capacity to place more effective and collectively determined limits on market activity. Despite the welcome constitutional reforms that some social democratic governments have managed to effect, its commitment to democracy remains too conventional and modest.

This leads on to a second set of issues surrounding the nature of community, which might be thought (if anything does) to distinguish social democracy from 'left liberalism'. Marquand (1999) has spoken of two differing orientations in (at least British) social democracy. One is value driven, the other largely 'technocratic'. The suspicion is that, in practice, the technocratic has come to prevail over the value driven. That is, social democracy has come to rely on a technical competence (formally through macro-economic management) to deliver desirable outcomes, rather than making the case for reform based on particular social values (autonomy, social justice, social solidarity). For a long time this technocratic 'substitutionism' could be seen as parasitic on an existing sense (and source) of community – whether in the nation-state or within what could once be called, without any sense of irony, the labour movement. In this sense, social democracy (in contrast to various forms of conservatism and neoliberalism) has been short on values. The resources of a shared identity on which social democracy once drew have become increasingly scarce, often giving way to a rather threadbare multiculturalism, a rather vague postmodernism or the attempt to squeeze just a little more out of the legacy of a lost world of labour.

But none of this will really do, because to function effectively social democracy, and especially social democracy in a cold climate, requires a fund of social solidarity. A number of social democratic politicians have recognized this but, as the short history of Tony Blair's encounter with 'community' suggests, these sorts of communal resources are extraordinarily difficult to create *ab initio*. In general, it is better to be lucky enough to find them than good enough to make them. In an 'anti-tax'/low-trust climate, smart social democrats may be able to 'do good by stealth' but only in a context where a growth dividend can obscure real patterns of redistribution. But a social democracy that cannot persuade the rich and resource-full that they *ought* to sanction transfers to the resource-poor is likely to prove increasingly ineffective, especially if growth slackens. Of course, social solidarity, like 'community', is not only something that politicians and policy-makers will always struggle to create, it is also far from unambiguously a 'good thing'. No community has a stronger sense of its own identity than the one which despises its neighbours. What social democrats really require is a kind of 'cosmopolitanism in one country'- though it remains quite unclear where this is to come from.

Both of these difficulties are greatly amplified when we shift our attention from individual states or from the club of affluent nations to include the much poorer majority of the world's population. Whatever uplifting noises it has made, with a few notable exceptions social democracy's internationalism has always been a rather flimsy affair. But even if social democrats choose not (very often) to think about their relationship to poorer parts of the planet, there is still an issue about the coordinated institutional response to the volatility of global markets (of the kind that rather latter-day interventionists, such as George Soros, have identified). We can certainly argue that, once again in social democracy's institutional heartland of Western and Northern Europe, supranational governance has made significant progress, largely at social democrats' behest. But, as experience in the European Union suggests, such institution-building can be slow and painful – and is likely to prove still more so in a global context of societies with very differing political institutions and levels of economic development.

There is one final issue that arises from the gaps left by the 'technocratic' and pragmatic orientation of traditional social democracy. This is the issue of ownership. Unfortunately, in recent years, this has been represented very largely as an issue of 'public ownership' versus privatization – a question that has been largely 'resolved' in favour of the latter. In fact, this is a relatively small, if consequential, corner of a much larger dispute. Schematically, Przeworski (1985) has written of the social democrats' 'discovery' of Keynes as conveniently resolving their traditional dilemma of how to expropriate the capitalist class without unleashing a social cataclysm. If Keynesianism meant that ownership no longer really mattered, it was an issue which social democrats could happily (and very conveniently) drop. But circumstances have changed and if there was a time when it could be said (plausibly if mistakenly) that 'ownership does not matter', such an argument could hardly be made now. In fact, in this area we have stepped backwards. Justifications of property and its distribution were at the heart of earlier arguments about the nature and legitimacy of the modern political order. A century ago, an inheritance tax, though fiercely condemned by some, was certainly a topic of polite debate among the mildly progressive – but even this now lies largely beyond the pale of polite conversation. In fact, the issue of why patterns of ownership (and the income streams associated with them) should be as they are is highly contentious. When thrust in front of social democratic policy-makers (as in the context of Aboriginal land rights) it causes acute embarrassment. The property question has not disappeared completely from social democratic discussion. It underpinned the wage-earners' fund initiative in Sweden in the 1970s and it is explicitly canvassed by the contemporary advocates of Basic Income (one more reason perhaps why this initiative lies at the fringes of current social democratic thought). Of course, for social democratic politicians who have spent much of their adult lifetime in the painstaking work of trying not to frighten voters, problematizing property rights belongs in the category of the *really* unthinkable and even more compellingly unsayable. But for those whose focus lies beyond the next election (or even the one after that) it is probably unavoidable.

These are issues vital to the future well-being of social democracy – to a politics that tries to build wide-ranging coalitions for the amelioration of inequality and the rectification of injustices.

But it is too much to expect that these ideas will originate from or, in the very near future, find a ready audience in Social Democratic parties. Those who stand outside the day-to-day business of social democratic governance face their own politics of creeping incrementalism, nudging the practitioners of 'nudge and fudge' in what they perceive to be the right direction. And whatever precisely is the shape of the 'new' social democracy to which this process gives rise, it will still be a politics of hard choices and messy outcomes.

Notes

Chapter 2   The Making of Social Democracy

The epigraphs come respectively from Kolakowski, cited in Owen, 1981, p. 67; Luxemburg, 1972, p. 50; Przeworski, 1985.

1   It is customary to describe Crosland's social democracy as 'revisionist' following his own usage and his explicit debt to Bernstein – 'the great socialist revisionist', in Crosland's account (1964, p. 62) – but it was much more the traditionalism of British socialism rather than Marxism which he sought to revise. Despite the commonalities, Crosland's conclusions (as well as many of his premises) differed significantly from those of Bernstein. Marxian revisionism was the source of one (or rather several) strands of later social democracy – but certainly not of its totality.

Chapter 3   'Classical' Social Democracy and the Alternatives

1   Przeworksi's *Capitalism and Social Democracy* (1985) sought to establish the implausibility of a 'parliamentary road to socialism' in terms of three strategic dilemmas faced by electoral socialists: whether to work for the advancement of socialism within or outside the existing institutions of capitalist society; whether to rely exclusively on the political backing of the working class or to seek multi- or even non-class support; and whether to press for reform of the existing socialist order or to dedicate all efforts and energies to the complete abolition of capitalism. In each instance, socialists chose

(perhaps unavoidably) to head down the social democratic road of participation. But the price of participation was the abandonment of even a moderate form of their final aims. *Controlling* the investment function *without* socializing ownership seemed to many social democrats to offer a neat way of resolving this dilemma. (For a fuller discussion, see C. Pierson, 1995, pp. 195–205.)

2 In the developed West, France was often described as having both the most underdeveloped social democratic tradition *and* the most developed apparatus for economic planning. On Britain, see Shaw, 1996, pp. 27–32.

3 In this context, it is worth remembering Karl Polanyi's insistence that, in some circumstances – and he was, after all, concerned with the rapid growth of market economies – it is only the *rate* rather than the *direction* of change that governments may affect, but that such intervention may be crucial in determining the social consequences of such change. (1944, pp. 36–8)

Chapter 4   Globalization and the End of Social Democracy

1 For an example of this slightly earlier redefinition of social democratic politics, see Gillespie and Paterson, 1993.

Chapter 5   The Challenge of Demographic Change

1 Where the aged dependency ratio reports the population over 64 as a percentage of the working age population.

2 The following section draws extensively on the criticism of *Averting the Old Age Crisis* originally published in the *International Social Security Review* in 1995 by R. Beattie and W. McGillivray, reprinted in Pierson and Castles, 2000.

Chapter 6   The Social Democratic Future

1 Although the issues are complex, it is hard to conceive of a 'real' equality of opportunity that did not also involve some increase in the equality of outcomes, not least because instituting a 'real' equality of opportunity requires resources.

2 Many of these policy innovations – including a major overhaul of the public service – were actually road-tested under the Hawke and Keating Labor governments in Australia during the 1980s and the first half of the 1990s, in a process that predated the election of Clinton by nearly a decade. Asked if this made him an originator of

the third way, Keating (1999) responded that he had seen the ALP's policy initiatives as 'the only way'.

3   Of course, the association between council house sales and working-class support for the Conservative Party is far from universally accepted; see Heath et al., 1991.

Bibliography

Aaron, H. J. 1966: 'The social insurance paradox', *Canadian Journal of Economics and Political Science*, 32 (Aug.), 371–4.

Abrams, M. and Rose, R. 1960: *Must Labour Lose?* Harmondsworth: Penguin.

Anderson, P. and Camiller, P. (eds) 1994: *Mapping the West European Left*. London: Verso.

Bale, T. 1999: 'The logic of no alternative? Political scientists, historians and the politics of Labour's past', *British Journal of Politics and International Relations*, 1, no. 2, 192–204.

Beattie, R. and McGillivray, W. 2000: 'On *Averting the Old Age Crisis*', in C. Pierson and F. G. Castles (eds), *The Welfare State Reader*, pp. 281–92. Cambridge: Polity.

Beilharz, P. 1994: *Transforming Labor: Labour Tradition and the Labor Decade in Australia*. Melbourne: Cambridge University Press.

Bernstein, E. 1909: *Evolutionary Socialism*. London: ILP.

Bernstein, E. 1993: *The Preconditions for Socialism*, ed. H. Tudor. Cambridge: Cambridge University Press.

Blackburn, R. 1999: 'The new collectivism: pension reform, grey capitalism and complex socialism', *New Left Review*, 233, 3–65.

Blair, Tony 1998: *The Third Way: New Politics for a New Century*. London: Fabian Society.

Boix, C. 1998: *Political Parties, Growth and Equality*. Cambridge: Cambridge University Press.

Bosworth, B. and Burtless, G. (eds) 1998: *Aging Societies: The Global Dimension*. Washington DC: Brookings Institution Press.

Bottomore, T. 1989: 'Austro-Marxist conceptions of the transition from capitalism to socialism', *International Journal of Comparative Sociology*, 30, nos 1–2, 109–20.

Burgmann, V. 1985: *In Our Time: Socialism and the Rise of Labor, 1885–1905*. Sydney: Allen and Unwin.

Cameron, D. R. 1978: 'The expansion of the public economy: a comparative analysis', *American Political Science Review*, 72, no. 4, 1243–61.

Castles, F. 1985: *The Working Class and Welfare*. Sydney: Allen and Unwin.

Castles, F. 1988: *Australian Public Policy and Economic Vulnerability*. Sydney: Allen and Unwin.

Castles, F. 1994: 'The wage earners' welfare state revisited: refurbishing the established model of Australian social protection, 1983–1993', *Australian Journal of Social Issues*, 29, no. 2, 120–45.

Castles, F. 1998: *Comparative Public Policy: Patterns of Post-war Transformation*. Cheltenham: Edward Elgar.

Castles, F. and Pierson, C. 1997: 'A new convergence? Recent policy developments in the UK, Australia and New Zealand', *Policy and Politics*, 24, no. 3, 233–245.

Castles, F., Gerritsen, R. and Vowles, J. 1996: *The Great Experiment: Labour Parties and Public Policy Transformation in Australia and New Zealand*. Sydney: Allen and Unwin.

Cerny, P. 1995: 'Globalization and the changing logic of collective action', *International Organization*, 49, no. 4, 595–625.

Childs, M. W. 1947: *Sweden: The Middle Way*. New Haven: Yale University Press.

Cline, W. R. 1997: *Trade and Wage Inequality*. Washington: Institute for International Economics.

Coates, D. 2000: *Models of Capitalism: Growth and Stagnation in the Modern Era*. Cambridge: Polity.

Commission on Social Justice 1994: *Social Justice*. London: Vintage.

Crosland, A. 1964: *The Future of Socialism* (1956). London: Cape.

de Beus, J. 1999: 'The politics of consensual well-being: the Dutch left greets the twenty-first century', in G. Kelly (ed.), *The New European Left*, pp. 59–68. London: Fabian Society.

Dean, M. 1998: 'Administering asceticism: reworking the ethical life of the unemployed citizen', in B. Hindess and M. Dean (eds), *Governing Australia*. Cambridge: Cambridge University Press.

DfEE (Department for Education and Employment, UK) 2000: *New Deal* (www.newdeal.gov.uk).

Dilnot, A., Disney, R., Johnson, P. and Whitehouse, E. 1994: *Pensions Policy in the UK: An Economic Analysis*. London: Institute for Fiscal Studies

Disney, R. 1996: *Can We Afford to Grow Older?* London: MIT Press.

Donnison, D. 1979: 'Social policy since Titmuss', *Journal of Social Policy*, 8, no. 2, 145–56.

Driver, S. and Martell, L. 1998: *New Labour Politics after Thatcherism*. Cambridge: Polity.

DSS (Department of Social Security, UK) 1999: *Partnership in Pensions*. London: HMSO.

Ebbinghaus, B. and Visser, J. 2000: *Trade Unions in Western Europe since 1945*. London: Macmillan.

Ellman, M. 1989: *Socialist Planning*, 2nd edn. Cambridge: Cambridge University Press.

Esping-Andersen, G. 1985: *Politics against Markets*. Princeton: Princeton University Press.

Esping-Andersen, G. 1990: *The Three Worlds of Welfare Capitalism*. Cambridge: Polity.

Esping-Andersen, G. (ed.) 1996: *Welfare States in Transition: National Adaptations in Global Economies*. London: Sage.

Finlayson, A. 1999: 'Third way theory', *Political Quarterly*, 70, no. 3, 271–9.

Fligstein, N. 1998: 'Is globalization the cause of the crises of welfare states', EUI Working Paper SPS 98/5, European University Institute, Florence.

Folbre, N. 1994: *Who Pays for the Kids? Gender and the Structures of Constraint*. London: Routledge.

Fougere, M. and Merette, M. 1999: 'Population ageing and economic growth in seven OECD countries', *Economic Modelling*, 16, 411–27.

Froebel, F., Heinrichs, J. and Kreile, O. 1980: *The New International Division of Labour*. Cambridge: Cambridge University Press.

Gamble, A. and Wright, A. (eds) 1999: *The New Social Democracy*. Oxford: Blackwell.

Garrett, G. 1998: *Partisan Politics in the Global Economy*. Cambridge: Cambridge University Press.

Garrett, G. 1999: 'Globalization and government spending around the world', working paper, Yale University (http://pantheon.yale.edu/~gmg8).

Garrett, G. 2000: 'Capital mobility, exchange rates and fiscal policy in the global economy', *Review of International Political Economy*, 7, no. 1, (Spring), 153–70.

Gay, P. 1952: *The Dilemma of Democratic Socialism*. New York: Octagon.

Giddens, A. 1990: *The Consequences of Modernity*. Cambridge: Polity.

Giddens, A. 1991: *Modernity and Self-Identity*. Cambridge: Polity.

Giddens, A. 1992: *The Transformation of Intimacy*. Cambridge: Polity.

Giddens, A. 1994: *Beyond Left and Right: The Future of Radical Politics.* Cambridge: Polity.

Giddens, A. 1998: *The Third Way: The Renewal of Social Democracy.* Cambridge: Polity.

Giddens, A. 1999: 'Politics after socialism' (http://www.lse.ac.uk/Giddens/pdf/03-feb-99.pdf).

Giddens, A. 2000: *The Third Way and its Critics.* Cambridge: Polity.

Giddens, A. and Pierson, C. 1999: *Making Sense of Modernity: Conversations with Giddens.* Cambridge: Polity.

Gillespie, R. and Paterson, W. E. 1993: *Rethinking Social Democracy In Western Europe.* London: Frank Cass.

Glyn, A. 1998: 'The assessment: economic policy and social democracy', *Oxford Review of Economic Policy,* 14, no. 1, (Spring), 1–18.

Golden, M. A., Wallerstein, M. and Lange, P. 1999: 'Postwar trade-union organization and industrial relations in twelve countries', in H. Kitschelt, P. Lange, G. Marks and J. Stephens (eds), *Continuity and Change in Contemporary Capitalism,* pp. 194–230. Cambridge: Cambridge University Press.

Golding, P. and Middleton, S. 1982: *Images of Welfare.* Oxford: Blackwell.

Goldthorpe, J. and Lockwood, D. 1969: *The Affluent Worker.* Cambridge: Cambridge University Press.

Goodin, R. E., Headley, B., Muffels, R. and Dirven, H.-J. 1999: *The Real Worlds of Welfare Capitalism.* Cambridge: Cambridge University Press.

Gorz, A. 1967: *Strategy for Labor.* Boston: Beacon.

Gray, J. 1993a: *Beyond the New Right.* London: Routledge.

Gray, J. 1993b: *Postliberalism.* London: Routledge.

Gray, J. 1996: *After Social Democracy: Politics, Capitalism and the Common Life.* London: Demos. Reprinted as chapter 2 in *Endgames,* Cambridge: Polity.

Gray, J. 1997: *Endgames.* Cambridge: Polity.

Gray, J. 1998: *False Dawn: The Delusions of Global Capitalism.* London: Granta.

Gruen, F. and Grattan, M. 1993: *Managing Government: Labor's Achievements and Failures.* Melbourne: Longman Cheshire.

Hall, P. A. (ed.) 1989: *The Political Power of Economic Ideas: Keynesianism across Nations.* Princeton: Princeton University Press.

Hay, C. 1997: 'Anticipating accommodations, accommodating anticipations: the appeasement of capital in the modernisation of the British Labour Party, 1987–92', *Politics and Society,* 25, no. 2, 234–56.

Hay, C. 1998: 'Globalization, welfare retrenchment and the logic of no alternative: why second-best won't do', *Journal of Social Policy*, 27, no. 4, 525–32.

Hay, C. 1999: *The Political Economy of New Labour*. Manchester: Manchester University Press.

Hay, C. 2000: 'Globalization, social democracy and the persistence of partisan politics: a commentary on Garrett', *Review of International Political Economy*, 7, no. 1 (Spring), 138–52.

Hayek, F. 1944: *The Road to Serfdom*. London: Routledge and Kegan Paul.

Heath, A. et al., 1991: *Understanding Political Change: The British Voter 1964–1987*. Oxford: Pergamon.

Held, D., McGrew, A., Goldblatt, D. and Perraton, J. 1999: *Global Transformations: Politics, Economics and Culture*. Cambridge: Polity.

Hills, J. 1997: *The Future of Welfare*, 2nd edn. York: LSE/Rowntree Trust.

Hirst, P. and Thompson, G. 1996: *Globalization in Question: The International Economy and the Possibilities of Governance*. Cambridge: Polity.

Hobsbawm, E. 1996: Jacket notes on D. Sassoon, *One Hundred Years of Socialism: The West European Left in the Twentieth Century*. London: I. B. Taurus.

ILO (International Labour Organization): *World Labour Report 1997/8* (www.ilo.org/public/english/dialogue/govlab/publ/wlr/97/index.htm).

Jacobs, M. 1999: 'Environmental democracy', in A. Gamble and A. Wright (eds), *The New Social Democracy*, pp. 105–16. Oxford: Blackwell.

Jacobzone, S., Cambois, E., Chaplain, E. and Robine, J. M. 1999: *The Health of Older Persons in OECD Countries*. Paris: OECD.

James, E. 2000: 'Social security around the world', in C. Pierson and F. G. Castles (eds), *The Welfare State Reader* pp. 271–80. Cambridge: Polity.

Jenkins, P. 1987: *Mrs Thatcher's Revolution*. London: Cape.

Jessop, B. 1994: 'The transition to post-Fordism and the Schumpeterian welfare state', in R. Burrows and B. Loader (eds), *Towards a Post-Fordist Welfare State?*, pp. 13–37. London: Routledge.

Jones, M. A. 1996: *The Australian Welfare State*, 4th edn. Sydney: Allen and Unwin.

Jospin, L. 1999: *Modern Socialism*. London: Fabian Society.

Katzenstein, P. 1985: *Small States in World Markets*. Ithaca, N.Y.: Cornell University Press.

Kautsky, K. 1910: *The Class Struggle*. New York: C. H. Kerr.

Kautsky, K. 1920: *Terrorism and Communism*. London: George Allen and Unwin.

Kautsky, K. 1964: *The Dictatorship of the Proletariat*. Ann Arbor: University of Michigan Press.

Keating, P. 1999: 'The Labour government 1983–1996', speech given at the University of New South Wales on 19 Mar. 1999 (www.keating.org.au).

Kelly, G. (ed.) 1999: *The New European Left*. London: Fabian Society.

Kelly, P. 1992: *The End of Certainty*. Sydney: Allen and Unwin.

Kelsey, J. 1995: *The New Zealand Experiment*. Auckland: Auckland University Press/Bridget Williams Books.

Kesselman, M. 1982: 'Prospects for democratic socialism in advanced capitalism: class struggle and compromise in Sweden and France', *Politics and Society*, 11, no. 4, 397–438.

Keynes, J. M. 1973: *The General Theory of Employment, Interest and Money*. London: Macmillan.

Kitschelt, H. 1994: *The Transformation of European Social Democracy*. Cambridge: Cambridge University Press.

Korpi, W. 1979: *The Working Class in Welfare Capitalism*. London: Routledge.

Korpi, W. 1983: *The Democratic Class Struggle*. London: Routledge.

Korpi, W. 1989: 'Power, politics and state autonomy in the development of social citizenship: social rights during sickness in eighteen OECD countries since 1930', *American Sociological Review*, 54, no. 3, 309–28.

Krieger, J. 1999: *British Politics in the Global Age: Can Social Democracy Survive?* Cambridge: Polity.

Krugman, P. 1994: 'Competitiveness: a dangerous obsession', *Foreign Affairs*, (Mar./Apr.), 28–44.

Lewis, J. 1998: ' "Work", "Welfare" and Lone Mothers', *Political Quarterly*, 16, no. 1, 4–13.

Lindblom, C. 1977: *Politics and Markets*. New York: Basic Books.

Lourdon, F. 1998: 'The logic and limits of désinflation compétitive', *Oxford Review of Economic Policy*, 14, no. 1, 96–113.

Luxemburg, R. 1970: *Reform or Revolution?* New York: Pathfinder.

Luxemburg, R. 1972: 'Social democracy and parliamentarism', in *Selected Political Writings*, ed. R. Looker. London: Cape.

McKay, A. 1998: 'Social security policy in Britain', in N. Ellison and C. Pierson (eds), *Developments in British Social Policy*, pp. 112–19. London: Macmillan.

Maddox, G. 1989: *The Hawke Government and Labor Tradition*. Ringwood: Penguin.

Marquand, D. 1984: *The Unprincipled Society: New Demands and Old Politics*. London: Cape.

Marquand, D. 1999: 'Premature obsequies: social democracy comes in from the cold', in A. Gamble and A. Wright (eds), *The New Social Democracy*, pp. 10–18. Oxford: Blackwell.

Marshall, T. H. 1963: *Sociology at the Crossroads* (1949). London: Heinemann.

Mead, L. 2000: 'The new politics of the new poverty', in C. Pierson and F. G. Castles (eds), *The Welfare State Reader*, pp. 107–17. Cambridge: Polity.

Michels, R. 1949: *Political Parties: A Sociological Study of the Oligarchical Tendencies of Modern Democracy*. Glencoe, Ill.: Free Press.

Middlemas, K. 1979: *Politics in Industrial Society: The experience of the British System since 1911*. London: Deutsch.

Miliband, R. 1961: *Parliamentary Socialism*. London: Allen and Unwin.

Miller, D. 1989: *Market, State and Community: Theoretical Foundations of Market Socialism*. Oxford: Clarendon.

Moran, M. 1999: *Governing the Health Care State*. Manchester: Manchester University Press.

Murray, C. 2000: 'The two wars against poverty', in C. Pierson and F. G. Castles (eds), *The Welfare State Reader*, pp. 96–106. Cambridge: Polity.

Nietzsche, F. 1996: *On the Genealogy of Morals*. Oxford: Oxford University Press.

Nove, A. 1983: *The Economics of Feasible Socialism*. London: Allen and Unwin.

O'Connor, J., Orloff, A. and Shaver, S. 1999: *States, Markets, Families: Gender, Liberalism and Social Policy in Australia, Canada, Great Britain and the United States*. Cambridge: Cambridge University Press.

OECD, 1988: *Reforming Public Pensions*. Paris: OECD.

OECD, 1992: *Private Pensions and Public Policy*. Paris: OECD.

OECD, 1994: *The Jobs Study*. Paris: OECD.

OECD, 1996: *Ageing in OECD Countries*. Paris: OECD.

OECD, 1997: *Family, Market and Community: Equity and Efficiency in Social Policy*. Paris: OECD.

OECD, 1998: *OECD Economic Outlook*, 63.

OECD, 1999: *A Caring World: The New Social Policy Agenda*. Paris: OECD.

Ohmae, K. 1990: *The Borderless World*. London: Collins.

Ohmae, K. 1995: *The End of the Nation State: The Rise of Regional Economies*. London: HarperCollins.

Orr, R. R. 1979: 'The neo-Idealist origins of British social democracy', Ph.D thesis, University of Maine, University Microfilms, Ann Arbor.

Owen, D. 1981: *Face the Future*. London: Cape.

Paine, T. 1985: *The Rights of Man*. Harmondsworth: Penguin.

Pateman, C. 1988: *The Sexual Contract.* Cambridge: Polity.

Perraton, J., Goldblatt, D., Held, D. and McGrew, A. 2000: 'Economic activity in a globalizing world', in D. Held and A. McGrew (eds), *The Global Transformations Reader,* pp. 287–300. Cambridge: Polity.

Pfaller, A., Gough, I. and Therborn, G. (eds) 1991: *Can the Welfare State Compete? A Comparative Study of Five Advanced Capitalist Countries.* London: Macmillan.

Phillipson, C. 2000: 'Intergenerational conflict and the welfare state: American and British perspectives', in C. Pierson and F. G. Castles (eds), *The Welfare State Reader,* pp. 294–307. Cambridge: Polity.

Pierson, C. 1986: *Marxist Theory and Democratic Politics.* Cambridge: Polity.

Pierson, C. 1995: *Socialism after Communism: The New Market Socialism.* Cambridge: Polity.

Pierson, C. 1998a: *Beyond the Welfare State,* 2nd edn. Cambridge: Polity.

Pierson, C. 1998b: 'Globalisation and the changing governance of welfare states: superannuation reform in Australia', *Global Society,* 12, no. 1, 31–47.

Pierson, C. 2000: 'The Australian model: old and new' (http://www.nottingham.ac.uk/politics/staff/pierson.html).

Pierson, C. and Castles, F. G. (eds) 2000: *The Welfare State Reader.* Cambridge: Polity.

Pierson, P. 1994: *Dismantling the Welfare State? Reagan, Thatcher, and the Politics of Retrenchment.* Cambridge: Cambridge University Press.

Pierson, P. 1996: 'The new politics of the welfare state', *World Politics,* 48, 143–79.

Pierson, P. 1998: 'Irresistible forces, immovable objects: post-industrial welfare states confront permanent austerity', *Journal of European Public Policy,* 5, no. 4, 539–60.

Pitruzzello, S. 1997: 'Social policy and the implementation of the Maastricht fiscal convergence criteria: the Italian and French attempts at welfare and pension reforms', *Social Research,* 64, no. 4.

Piven, F. F. 1992: *Labor Parties in Postindustrial Societies.* New York: Oxford University Press.

Plant, R. 1996: 'Social democracy', in D. Marquand and A. Seldon (eds), *The Ideas that Shaped Post-war Britain.* London: HarperCollins.

Plant, R. 1998: 'The third way', Friedrich-Ebert-Stiftung Working Papers 5/98, London.

Polanyi, K. 1944: *The Great Transformation.* New York: Rinehart.

Pontusson, J. 1995: 'Explaining the decline of European social democracy', *World Politics,* 47, no. 4, 495–533.

Pontusson, J. and Swenson, P. 1996: 'Labor markets, production strategies, and wage bargaining institutions: the Swedish employer offensive in comparative perspective', *Comparative Political Studies*, 29, no. 2, 223–50.

Progressive Foundation 1996: *The New Progressive Declaration*. Washington DC: Progressive Foundation.

Przeworski, A. 1985: *Capitalism and Social Democracy*. Cambridge: Cambridge University Press.

Przeworski, A. and Wallerstein, M. 1988: 'Structural dependence of the state on capital', *American Political Science Review*, 82, 11–30.

Razin, A. and Sadka, E. 1999: 'Migration and pension with international capital mobility', *Journal of Public Economics*, 74, no. 1, 141–50.

Rhodes, M. 1998: 'Globalization, labour markets and welfare states: a future of "competitive corporatism"', in M. Rhodes and Y. Meny, *The Future of European Welfare*, pp. 178–203. London: Macmillan.

Rieger, E. and Leibfried, S. 1998: 'Welfare state limits to globalization', *Politics and Society*, 26, no. 3, 363–90.

Rodrik, D. 1997: *Has Globalization Gone Too Far?* Washington DC: Institute for International Economics.

Roemer, J. E. 1994: *A Future for Socialism*. Cambridge, Mass.: Harvard University Press.

Rosselli, C. 1994: *Liberal Socialism* (1930). Princeton: Princeton University Press.

Royal Commission on Population 1949: *Report*. London: HMSO.

Ryner, M. J. 1998: *Neoliberal Globalization and the Crisis of Swedish Social Democracy*. Florence: European University Institute.

Salvadori, M. 1979: *Karl Kautsky and the Socialist Revolution: 1880–1938*. London: New Left Books.

Saraceno, C. 1997: 'Family change, family policies and the restructuring of welfare', in P. Hennessy and M. Pearson (eds), *Family, Market and Community*. Paris: OECD.

Sassoon, D. 1996: *One Hundred Years of Socialism: The West European Left in the Twentieth Century*. London: I. B. Taurus.

Sauvy, A. 1969: *General Theory of Population*. London: Weidenfeld and Nicholson.

Scharpf, F. W. 1991: *Crisis and Choice in European Social Democracy*. London: Cornell University Press.

Scherer, P. 1996: 'The myth of the demographic imperative', in C. E. Steuerle and M. Kawai (eds), *The New World Fiscal Order*. Washington: Urban Institute Press.

Schmidt, M. 1983: The welfare state and the economy in periods of economic crisis: a comparative study of 23 OECD countries', *European Journal of Political Research*, 17, no. 6, 641–59.

Schwartz, H. 1998: 'Social democracy going down vs. social democracy down under? Institutions, internationalized capital, and indebted states', *Comparative Politics*, 30, no. 3.

Schwartz, H. 2000a: 'Internationalization and two welfare states: Australia and New Zealand', in F. Scharpf and V. Schmidt (eds), *Welfare and Work in the Open Economy*, vol. 2. Oxford: Oxford University Press.

Schwartz, H. 2000b: 'Round up the usual subjects! Globalization, domestic politics and welfare state change', in P. Pierson (ed.), *The New Politics of the Welfare State*. Oxford: Oxford University Press.

Selucky, R. 1979: *Marxism, Socialism, Freedom: Towards a General Democratic Theory of Labour-Managed Systems*. London: Macmillan.

Shaw, E. 1996: *The Labour Party since 1945*. Oxford: Blackwell.

Skidelsky, R. 1979: 'The decline of Keynesian politics', in C. Crouch (ed.), *State and Economy in Contemporary Capitalism*, pp. 55–87. London: Croom Helm.

Snowdon, B. and Vane, H. R. (eds) 1997: *A Macroeconomics Reader*. London: Routledge.

Socialist International 1999: *Declaration of Principles* (http://www.socialistinternational.org/4principles/dofpeng.html).

Soskice, D. 1999: 'Divergent production regimes: coordinated and uncoordinated market economies in the 1980s and 1990s', in H. Kitschelt, P. Lange, G. Marks and J. Stephens (eds), *Continuity and Change in Contemporary Capitalism*, pp. 101–34. Cambridge: Cambridge University Press.

Steger, M. B. 1997: *The Quest for Evolutionary Socialism: Edward Bernstein and Social Democracy*. Cambridge: Cambridge University Press.

Strange, S. 1994: *States and Markets*. London: Pinter.

Strange, S. 1996: *The Retreat of the State: The Diffusion of Power in the World Economy*. Cambridge: Cambridge University Press.

Swank, D. 1998a: 'Funding the welfare state: globalization and the taxation of business in advanced market economies', *Political Studies*, 46, no. 4, 671–92.

Swank, D. 1998b: 'Global capital, democracy, and the welfare state: why political institutions are so important in shaping the domestic response to internationalization', Political Economy of European Integration Working Paper 1.66, University of California Center for German and European Studies, Berkeley.

Taylor-Gooby, P. 1999: 'Policy change at a time of retrenchment: recent pension reform in France, Germany, Italy and the UK', *Social Policy and Administration*, 33, no. 1, 1–19.

Teeple, G. 1995: *Globalization and the Decline of Social Reform*. Toronto: Garamond Press.

Therborn, G. 1987: 'Welfare states and capitalist markets', *Acta Sociologica*, 30, nos 3–4, 237–54.

Tilton, T. 1990: *Swedish Social Democracy*. Oxford: Oxford University Press.

van Kersbergen, K. 1995: *Social Capital*. London: Routledge

van Parijs, P. 1995: *Real Freedom for All: What (If Anything) Can Justify Capitalism?* Oxford: Oxford University Press.

van Parijs, P. (ed.) 1992: *Arguing for a Basic Income*. London: Verso.

Visser, J. 1998: 'Two cheers for corporatism, one for the market: industrial relations, wage moderation and job growth in the Netherlands', *British Journal of Industrial Relations*, 36, no. 2, 269–92.

Waine, B. 1995: 'A disaster foretold? The case of the personal pension', *Social Policy and Administration*, 29, no. 4, 317–44.

Walzer, M. 1983: *Spheres of Justice*. Oxford: Martin Robertson.

White, S. 1997: 'Liberal equality, exploitation and the case for an unconditional basic income', *Political Studies*, 45, no. 2, 312–26.

White, S. 1998a: 'Interpreting the "third way": not one route, but many' (http://www.netnexus.org/library/papers/white2.htm).

White, S. 1998b: 'Third way and all that' (http://www.netnexus.org/mail_archive/uk-policy.3way/0076.html).

Wiseman, J. 1996: 'A kinder road to hell? Labor and the politics of progressive competitiveness in Australia', *Socialist Register*, 93–117.

World Bank, 1994: *Averting the Old Age Crisis*. New York: Oxford University Press.

Index